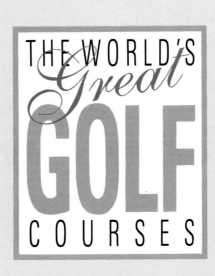

THE WORLD'S
Great
GOLF
COURSES

THE WORLD'S
Great
GOLF
COURSES

MICHAEL HOBBS

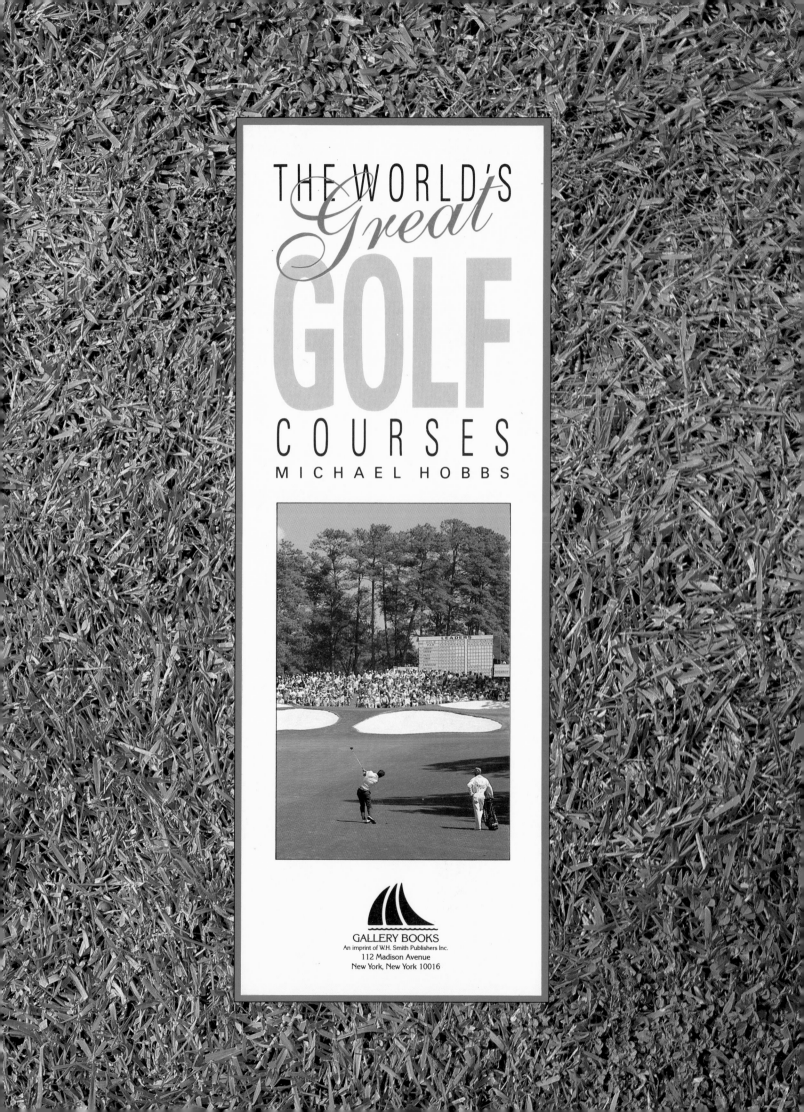

GALLERY BOOKS
An imprint of W.H. Smith Publishers Inc.
112 Madison Avenue
New York, New York 10016

For Margaret

A QUINTET BOOK
produced for
GALLERY BOOKS
An imprint of W.H. Smith Publishers Inc.
112 Madison Avenue
New York, New York 10016

ISBN 0-8317-3909-6

This book was designed and produced by
QUINTET PUBLISHING LIMITED
6 Blundell Street
London N7 9BH

ART DIRECTOR: Peter Bridgewater
DESIGNER: Linda Henley
EDITORS: Paul Barnett, Judith Simons

Typeset in Great Britain by
Central Southern Typesetters, Eastbourne
Manufactured in Hong Kong by Regent Publishing Services Limited
Printed in Hong Kong by Leefung-Asco Printers Limited

● PICTURE CREDITS ●

Key: *t* = top; *b* = bottom; *l* = left; *r* = right.

The author and publishers had made every effort to identify the copyright owners of the pictures used in this publication; they apologize for any omissions and would like to thank the following:

ALL-SPORT (UK) LTD: pages 14 *b*, 15, 18/9, 19 *b*, 34/5, 35 *b*, 42, 42–4, 48–9, 54, 63, 67, 73 *r*, 76, 87 *t*, 91–3, 95, 98, 105 *b* (photos David Cannon); 16/7 (photo Adrian Murrell); 56/7, 105 *t*, 109 *t*, 109 *t*. PETER DAZELEY: pages 3, 12/3, 13, 14 *t*, 26/7, 27, 45 *b*, 68/9, 74–5, 81, 82/3, 88–9, 94/5, 99. COURSEGUIDE PUBLICATIONS LTD: pages 17 *t*. COURTESY THE GLENEAGLES HOTEL: page 30. MICHAEL HOBBS COLLECTION: pages 6–9, 17 *b*, 19 *t*, 20 *l*, 21 *b*, 25 *b*, 29 *r*, 31, 40–1, 45 *t*, 46-7, 51 *b*, 53 *b*, 55, 57, 59–62, 66 *b*, 68, 73 *l*, 77, 79, 85 *t b*, 86, 90/1, 96, 103, 106–7, 109 *b*. COURTESY INVERNESS CLUB: page 35 *t* (photo J Brune). COURTESY JAGORAWI GOLF AND COUNTRY CLUB: page 36/7. © LEONARD KAMSLER: pages 24, 25 *t*, 50/1, 51 *t*. COURTESY PEBBLE BEACH COMPANY: pages 64/5, 66 *t*. COURTESY OF PINEHURST HOTEL AND COUNTRY CLUB: pages 7–1. © TONY ROBERTS: pages 20 *r*, 21 *t* 22/3, 38–9, 52/3, 53 *t*, 54/5, 56, 97. COURTESY ROYAL ST GEORGE'S GOLF CLUB: pages 84/5, 87 *b*. © SATOUR: page 28/9. COURTESY SEA PINES RESORTS: pages 11, 32–3. © PATRICK SQUIRE: page 28 *t b*. COURTESY SUN INTERNATIONAL (BOPHUTHATSWANA) LTD: page 100/1. COURTESY VENICE SIMPLON ORIENT-EXPRESS HOTELS: pages 102/3, 104/5.

● CONTENTS ●

INTRODUCTION

The earliest golf courses ('links') were alongside the Scottish coasts, and they were born from a combination of the workings of nature and the choices of men. Some of the early centres of golf were Leith, Musselburgh, Dornoch, St Andrews and Montrose. The people who came to play over the land had no thoughts of shaping it. Originally players simply agreed beforehand the route they would take and it was some time before the idea of fixed positions for the greens took on. Tees, of course, were a much later idea. In the early days of golf, you holed your ball, took a few steps away and then hit off towards the next green.

The route from green to green was dictated by nature – between the dunes and furze, with possibly an occasional shot sent soaring over the top of a dune. With grass-cutting machines still to be invented, rabbits and sheep did the job on linksland. Inland golf, on courses such as at Perth in Scotland, was possible only outside the main growing season: in late spring and high summer grass grows too fast for animals to crop it short.

The first endeavours to change the natural state of the land came around the middle of the last century. Up to this time greens had been extremely variable in their surfaces. Cutting and simple feeding began – Old Tom Morris, for example, believed that scattering sand was a cure for most ills. At much the same time, the first bunkers (sandtraps) were dug to make hitherto easy shots more difficult.

Inland golf became possible with improved grass-cutting machinery. Some of the world's great golf courses are largely natural, but others are almost entirely the work of the architect's mind and of the machines which carry out his design. As the land often lacked the natural bumps and hollows of linksland, people began to create features, first using spades and horse-drawn tools and then later with earth-moving machinery. Today, creating a top-level golf course involves changing the whole shape of the landscape. Valleys are sculpted, hills pushed up, rocks blasted, swamps drained and rivers diverted. It is an expensive activity.

Golf courses are set on terrain as various as nature itself. In this book you will find courses

LEFT A typical expanse of fine linksland. The sea, the stabilized dunes and the humpy ground give this kind of golf much of its character.

ABOVE On this severely contoured green there is a significant fall from where the golfer has taken his stance down to the flag. Judgement of pace has to be subtle.

TOP LEFT In the early days of golf, no one thought of using wooded country for the game. Later, architects such as Harry Colt began to cut courses through woodland, although there can be severe drainage problems.

ABOVE The humps and hollows at the approaches to this green mean that a ball pitching short could go anywhere!

carved through forests or ranging across windswept links where no trees could survive. Others run along clifftops or are down at sea-level on land once occupied by swamps or salt marshes. And others were created on rich farmland or on acid heaths and moorlands where no crops have ever grown.

Although the great courses can be found in all these varied settings, they have many 'ingredients' in common that make them a supreme test and a delight. What are these ingredients? In the first place, beauty. Golf is alone among the major sports in taking place in surroundings that are always pleasant and often stunning. The great courses are not only superb places to play golf but a joy to visit.

Many of the most famous are widely known because they host tournaments and the great championships. For this kind of play, many factors operate besides the sheer quality of the golf. There must be room for car parking, plenty of hotel accommodation, and centres of population close at hand so that the crowds will come to watch. Those spectators need a course where there are natural viewing points and space to move around following the players.

No course is considered for a major event unless its total length is more than 6,500 yards (5,940 m) and preferably close to 7,000 yards (6,400 m). Yet ordinary club members and visiting golfers do not demand or even welcome the monster course. So there are some great golf

courses that may never host a championship but nevertheless are capable of testing a player's abilities with every club in the bag. Should some holes demand superhuman shots, the moderate golfer should be offered an alternative route: a 220-yard (200-m) par 3 with a green in the middle of a lake is not a good golf hole!

One cannot expect all 18 holes of a golf course to be great, but some at least should cause a tingle of anticipation, perhaps even fear. It is equally important that there should be as few poor holes as possible. When the architect of the past had to use the landscape as it existed, three or four poor holes among the 18 were almost inevitable, but this happens far less often now that machines can create features where

none existed before.

Greens are where about half the shots in a game are played. It goes without saying that the surfaces should be true. Contouring should be subtle rather than extravagant and, even after much rain, the greens should remain fast. In average conditions they should hold the well struck shot while allowing others to drift away to bunkers or with the flow of the ground.

The courses chosen for this book all have these qualities and many more, but they remain very much my personal choices. Few readers, I think, will quarrel with any of the golf courses I have included; many will protest the exclusion of others. After all, doesn't every golfer think his or her own course the best in the world?

ABOVE If you are not enjoying your game, pause to enjoy the views. They can be truly spectacular as here at Lahinch, County Clare, Ireland.

THE GOLF COURSES

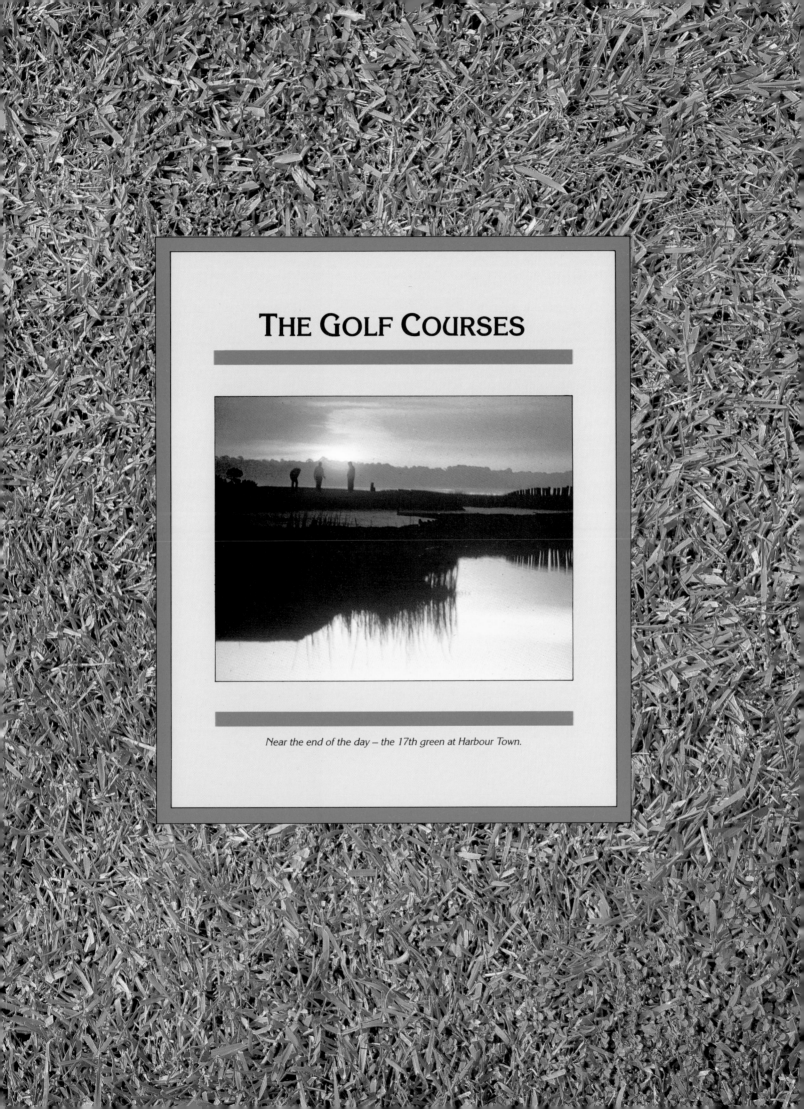

Near the end of the day — the 17th green at Harbour Town.

AUGUSTA

When the course at Killarney, Ireland, became the passion of Viscount Castlerosse towards the end of his life, he hired a skilled horticulturist to design him the perfect plant scheme so that the course would be in bloom every day of the year. The plans were produced but never put into practice, owing to Castlerosse's death early in World War II. What Castlerosse had in mind was Augusta – the world's best known golf course – in the spring at Masters time.

Castlerosse was an early admirer of the course. It was to be many more years before Augusta, particularly the last nine holes, became familiar worldwide. This came with the arrival of television in the mid-1950s, only a short time after the Masters had become recognized as a major title (it is not a championship of anywhere or anything). Some say that this recognition came immediately after World War II; others that the 1954 play-off between the two greatest players of the day, Sam Snead and Ben Hogan, was what brought it about. Whatever the truth of the matter, the players had long regarded the tournament as well above all the rest on the US Tour except for the two championships. With the passing of the years, the Masters title has become as desirable as those of the British and US Opens.

The Augusta course was originally Fruitland Nurseries, founded in 1857 by Baron Louis Berckmans. Bobby Jones, after he had won the Open and Amateur Championships of both the United States and Great Britain in 1930, wanted to be involved in creating a championship course in the American South. In 1929, over on the West Coast to play the US Amateur at Pebble Beach, he had also played Cypress Point and been highly impressed. The architect there had been Dr Alister Mackenzie. A couple of years later, a civic leader in Augusta, Georgia, wanted to promote the town to encourage visitors, and he is said to have suggested that the nursery might make a golf course. Clifford Roberts, later to mastermind the Masters for over 40 years, saw the property and later took Jones along. Both felt it had superb possibilities, and the combination of Mackenzie and Jones was at work by 1931. Jones did not think of himself as the designer in any sense but he did hit hundreds

AUGUSTA NATIONAL GOLF CLUB
AUGUSTA, GEORGIA
UNITED STATES

RIGHT Augusta's magnificent clubhouse is of comparable age to the Royal and Ancient Golf Club's home at St Andrews, Scotland. It dates from before the Civil War.

ABOVE FAR RIGHT A practice day scene at the Masters. These competitors are on the 18th tee.

of shots to help decide where tees, greens and bunkers should be sited to test the best players, and no doubt he also expressed many opinions to Mackenzie.

The course they arrived at is still close to unique in being a frightener for very good players yet a course where handicap players who know their limitations may well score better than on their home course. Bunkering, for example, is not severe. There were not many more than 20 on the original course, and that number has only doubled over the 50 years since then. Those flanking fairways were a threat only to long hitters out beyond 200 yards (180 m). Water hazards, too, were more in play for those trying to reach par 5s in two than modest players expecting to pitch on – except, many may say, the par-3 16th, much less menacing to handicap players in the original design of the hole than it is now. Then there is the rough – or, more accurately, the lack of it: if you cannot find your ball at Augusta you just didn't see where it went!

In short, although the course allows – even helps – moderate players to enjoy themselves, it is one of the great tests of the best players. Why? In part it is due to the extreme pace and contouring of the greens. The shot in to the green must be well placed to give a birdie chance, and it is usually desperately difficult to get a long approach putt close to the hole. The course also favours long hitters who can carry the rises of

PRIOR	HOLE	1	2	3	4	5	6	7	8	9	10	11	12	13	14	15	16	17	18
	PAR	4	5	4	3	4	3	4	5	4	4	4	3	5	4	5	3	4	4
0	WEISKOPF	0	1	0	0	1	1	1	0	1	1	1	2	2	2	2	1		
3	BARBER M.	3	3	2	2	2	2	1	0	0	1	1	2	2	3	3	3	2	
1	FUNSETH	1	0	0	1	1	1	1	2	2	1	2	2	3	4	4	5	5	
2	TREVINO	2	3	3	3	4	4	4	4	5	4	4	4	4	4	4			
0	ARMSTRONG	0	0	0	1	2	2	2	2	2	2	2	3	3	4	3			
0	THOMPSON	0	1	1	1	1	0	0	0	0	0	0	2	2					
4	SCHLEE	3	4	3	2	2	2	2	3	1	1	1	1						
1	WATSON	2	2	1	0	0	1	1	1	1	1	1	2	2					
1	IRWIN	1	0	1	0	1	1	1	2	1	2	1	2	2	2	3	4		
0	LITTLER	0	1	1	1	1	1	2	2	2	3	3	4	4	4	4	4		

THRU 14 WATSON 2 PLAYER 1

THRU 3 INMAN 2 PALMER 2 JANUARY 2

ABOVE Tom Watson waits to play as Gary Player stoops to retrieve the ball.

RIGHT Although Jack Nicklaus will never rank as one of the great bunker players, he certainly learned to be good enough. He has now been the Masters champion on a record six occasions.

first nine, mainly as a result of the fact that four shots to the green have to be played over water.

Nevertheless there is nothing too wrong with what are today Augusta's first nine. Here Seve Ballesteros made one of the great bursts of major golf on 19 April 1983 – with a start of birdie, eagle, par, birdie – which thrust him to the front of the field in the final round. Generally speaking, the first half of the course yields fewer clear-cut birdie opportunities, but fewer titles are lost here.

The second nine begins with one of the sternest holes at Augusta. If the 13th is a very short par 5, the 10th makes up for this by being possibly the longest par 4 in the world – 485 yards (443 m). However, there is plenty of run for the tee shot if the player keeps left along the fairway, which is also the shortest line to the green. Although Jones and Mackenzie are rightly credited with the design of the course, this hole was much improved before World War II when architect Perry Maxwell moved the green from low ground to its present elevated position. The 11th was improved at the same time, and at some 450 yards (410 m) needs a long second shot – perilous as the flag is set well left with water hard by that side of the green.

ground at some holes, who fly the ball high, and who draw the ball. Trevino hates the course, yet Nicklaus, who has almost always tried to play moving the ball left to right, just like Trevino, has performed brilliantly here, winning a record six Masters. To play Augusta superbly, you need to drive long and high, have perfect touch for long putts and chips, and be very resolute in holing the short but missable putts.

The first hole Jones and Mackenzie 'found' at Augusta was, apparently, what is now the 13th. Most course designers see a few holes they think would be superb and then try to make the rest fit in. The 13th is a very short par 5 indeed, at just 465 yards (425 m) (under British regulations it would be a par 4). Ideally, you draw the ball from the tee around the angle, menaced by an innocent-seeming creek, and with your second carry that same creek as it curls in front of the green. If that really was the first hole 'discovered' then the discovery was a great one, a hole that rewards two well played shots with a certain birdie but is an easy par for a competent handicap player – or a disaster if you find the creek with your tee shot or close to the green.

Originally, this hole was the 4th, because what is now the testing championship stretch to the finish constituted the first nine holes. Then it was realized how much drama was included in the

The 12th, a par 3 of 155 yards (142 m), provokes perhaps more doubt in the player's mind than any other hole of the course. Rae's Creek runs across the front of the green, which has little depth to it. If you play safe with a long shot you risk landing in the bunkers at the rear of the green, with a dangerous shot back in the direction of the creek. The water's threat is greatest to the tee shot when the flag is set well right, which lengthens the carry so that the player has little more than a 10-yard (9-m) margin between success and disaster. Tom Kite lost the 1984 Masters when he took 6 on this hole while Ben Crenshaw went on to win after a 2. Kite later commented that choice of club is a matter of total guesswork on this hole, because of the winds that swirl above the trees behind the green.

The par 5s are often the key to a low round at Augusta. As we have seen, if the tee shot is drawn around the angle at the 13th, prospects of being on in two are excellent, but Rae's Creek is still a threat, both in front of the green and then swerving around the right-hand side. Jones called it 'one of the finest holes for competitive play I have seen'.

The next par 5, the 15th, is some 50 yards (46 m) longer, but the tee shot looks very inviting. Even so, line is important, the right-centre giving more run and a better line to the green. A really big drive may leave you with something like a 4-iron shot in to the green. If you overclub, or if you shut the face a little (as Larry Mize did in the 1987 Masters), it is easy to run through the green and on to the pond on the 16th. Best of all, then, is to hole your second shot, as Gene Sarazen did in the 1935 Masters – which enabled him to tie with Craig Wood and then go on to win the play-off the next day.

The dramas are not over! The 16th, a medium length par 3, has water all the way from in front of the tee to the green and even then along the green's left-hand side. Nevertheless, the hole has certainly been kind to Jack Nicklaus. It was the key to his winning the 1975 Masters, when he holed a vast putt for a 2, and in 1986 he played a spectacular tee shot that might easily have been a hole in one.

The finish is not quite up to the standard of what has gone before – yet it should not be underestimated. A Masters player who is a stroke in the lead at this point thinks he needs merely to par both the closing par 4s to wrap up the title. Yet neither is by any means easy, the 17th being the hole most open to criticism on

the course because the second shot is semi-blind even after a good tee shot. The 18th has seen many dramas over the years, and a shot towards the rear of the long green when the pin is set more to the front very often leads to three putts; Ben Hogan lost the 1946 Masters this way. By contrast, Gary Player holed a very good down-hiller in 1978 and later emerged the champion.

Augusta may be neither the most beautiful nor the best course in the world, but there is no obvious candidate that one could prefer to it. Its condition may be unparalleled in part because it is so little played. There are few members, most of whom live far away, and even a Masters champion cannot invite a friend or two along for a game. With even tickets to watch the Masters virtually unobtainable, you can imagine how difficult it is for a golfer to have a chance to play the course!

ABOVE Although many fairways are tree-lined at Augusta, amazing recoveries are possible since players can often find a way through the trees instead of having to chip out sideways.

THE AUSTRALIAN

THE AUSTRALIAN
GOLF CLUB
KENSINGTON, SYDNEY
NEW SOUTH WALES
AUSTRALIA

RIGHT A fish-eye lens captures some of the feeling of tournament play at The Australian, Sydney. Note the vast bunkers and the threat of water.

As with the United States, England and numerous other countries, it was Scots or people of Scottish descent who brought golf to Australia. Credit is sometimes given to James Graham from Fife, Scotland. He began organizing a little golf in Melbourne in the late 1840s, while John Dunsmore played in Sydney a few years later. However, Alex Reid introduced the game down south in Tasmania during the 1830s, and was in at the foundation of Australia's oldest club, Bothwell, which claims 1830 as its birth date.

The Australian can certainly claim to have been there at the beginning of the explosion of golf popularity in the country. As in England and the United States — and even, for that matter, Scotland — this was at the end of the 1880s. The club was founded in 1882, but lost its course a few years later. The present course dates from 1902, but has been much altered over the years. Dr Alister Mackenzie did some work in the late 1920s, while Jack Nicklaus designed new holes in 1977. Besides setting bunkers in the drive area at most holes, Nicklaus greatly increased the influence of water hazards on the course. Nicklaus has the distinction of having won the Australian Open on the previous lay-out in 1975 and 1976 and again in 1978 after the changes had been made. This was the last of his six

Australian Open victories.

The course was first used for the Australian Open in 1920 and, as the best tournament course in the Sydney area, has been the venue for it many times since. It is an excellent choice because there are many vantage points from which spectators can look down on the action, while for the performers themselves the course is one of the most testing in the country. The hazards are well placed to take account of the modern ball and equipment. At over 7,100 yards (6,490 m) it is certainly long enough!

The first few holes do not demand great length for the shot to the green, but thereafter the long par 4s dominate the course, some being unreachable if you are playing into anything more than a breeze. The finish is as it should be, the most demanding and challenging section of the Australian.

Many people find the three holes immediately prior to the last the most challenging. The 15th is just over 200 yards (183 m), with the green almost an island surrounded by sand. The 16th causes considerable irritation: many shots which find the green at this 400-yard (365-m) hole bound through – only a superbly struck shot will hold.

The 17th, measuring about 430 yards (390 m), may be the most difficult on the course. The long second shot has to carry water – often into the wind. However, the last hole, a par 5, offers a do-or-die chance of being up in two but has an expanse of water in wait to the right of the green for those who fail.

ABOVE A view of the 4th hole. When Jack Nicklaus made his design changes in 1977, he brought water much more into play.

LEFT Norman von Nida was the best Australian golfer for several years following World War II. A very straight hitter, he was also superb from sand – and much more variable on the greens. Von Nida was always ready to help and advise a succession of talented young Australians, including Greg Norman.

BALLYBUNION OLD

BALLYBUNION GOLF CLUB
COUNTY KERRY
IRELAND

RIGHT Nearing home at the end of the day, the 17th green is a superb golf hole and the real climax of the round.

FAR RIGHT Many shots to the short 8th find sand and the recovery shot can easily overrun the green into yet more trouble.

BELOW RIGHT The 5th green used to end a round at Ballybunion before the routing of the course was changed. The village is a popular holiday destination.

That a course is used for major championships does not necessarily mean that it is one of the great ones. Ballybunion, on the Shannon Estuary in the west of Ireland, is remote from large population centres. As a result, no great championship is ever likely to come here, but the two courses are still among the world's greatest. Between them they provide perhaps the best 36 holes of true links golf in the world. If you could play a game on the best 18 holes of the 36, there is no doubt at all that you would be playing the best links course anywhere – every hole demanding, yet all of them fair.

Today, Ballybunion Old ranks, at worst, among the world's top 20 courses. Little more than 20 years ago it was known to only the locals and the well informed. Herbert Warren Wind was perhaps the man initially responsible for changing all this. He came to Ballybunion in the 1960s and went away saying: 'Very simply, Ballybunion revealed itself to be nothing less than the finest seaside course I have ever seen.' He wrote at length about it in the United States, and the news slowly spread. Since then, Tom Watson has preached the Ballybunion gospel: 'A man would think the game of golf began here.' Watson, at times a severe critic of present-day architects, also wrote: 'Ballybunion is a course on which many golf architects should live and play before they build golf courses.' Watson liked the wild contours and the relative absence of blind shots on such a primeval course. He appreciated the way that at Ballybunion iron shots must find not only the green but the *right area* of the green if they are not to squirt away sideways. Also he liked the fact that short or slightly long shots are less severely punished than those that miss to right or left.

The start of the Old is not severe, a par 4 of less than 400 yards (365 m) partly alongside a road and a graveyard. The first few holes are fairly flat and uninteresting except the 2nd, which is just about the most testing of the entire course. The drive is uphill, and then the second shot must fly between two humps and carry to a green on the top of a ridge. The 4th and 5th, when they were the 17th and 18th, used to make people shake their heads. They are flat and uninspiring and, before the new clubhouse was

built in the 1970s so that the order of playing the holes changed, made for a dull finish to the course. They are much more acceptable holes now they are positioned early on.

After the 5th, the real Ballybunion begins. The 6th, with its narrow green right by the sea, demands a very precise iron shot in and, into the wind, plays far longer than its 360 yards (330 m). The 7th, well over 400 yards (365 m), plays all along the sea cliff, with no hope for the slicer. There follows one of Ballybunion's strengths, a really great par 3. From a tee that backs onto the ocean the flag is only 150 yards (135 m) or so away, but it has been claimed that even Tom Watson could find no shot in his armoury which would hold the green. The ground falls away rapidly to either side, and so you might do better to finish in sand.

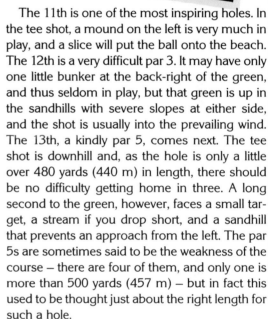

The 11th is one of the most inspiring holes. In the tee shot, a mound on the left is very much in play, and a slice will put the ball onto the beach. The 12th is a very difficult par 3. It may have only one little bunker at the back-right of the green, and thus seldom in play, but that green is up in the sandhills with severe slopes at either side, and the shot is usually into the prevailing wind. The 13th, a kindly par 5, comes next. The tee shot is downhill and, as the hole is only a little over 480 yards (440 m) in length, there should be no difficulty getting home in three. A long second to the green, however, faces a small target, a stream if you drop short, and a sandhill that prevents an approach from the left. The par 5s are sometimes said to be the weakness of the course – there are four of them, and only one is more than 500 yards (457 m) – but in fact this used to be thought just about the right length for such a hole.

A short par 3, uphill, follows and then another – an unorthodox sequence of three par 3s in four holes. The last of them, the 15th, is a great hole. About 200 yards (180 m) in length, with humps and bunkers crowding the putting area and a large mound in front of the two-tiered green to the left, you can be supremely satisfied if you find the green. The 16th and 17th both have sharp doglegs to the left, played between the dunes with the drive at the 17th being played from a high tee. The last hole is not so fine. Good players have to drive short of a vast bunker some 250 yards (230 m) away and then play a blind pitch to the narrow green.

After the 18 holes of the Old the golfer can retreat to the clubhouse or embark on a journey among the even wilder dunes of Robert Trent Jones's New course. This one can be just too difficult for moderate players a little off their game, the shots to the green sometimes leaving little margin between success and catastrophe.

BALTUSROL GOLF CLUB
SPRINGFIELD
NEW JERSEY
UNITED STATES

ABOVE The present courses at Baltusrol were constructed after World War I. Ed Furgol plays the winning putt for the US Open title in 1954 – the first time the championship was held on the Lower course.

BALTUSROL LOWER COURSE

Baltusrol has two splendid courses lying at the bottom of one of the Watchung Mountains. It takes its name from a certain Dutch farmer, Baltus Roll, who was bludgeoned to death by two thieves who believed that he kept all his cash in the house.

That was in 1831. In 1895, a nine-hole course was created and, by the time the United States entered World War I, two US Opens had been played here, won by Willie Anderson (1903) and Jerry Travers (1915). After that war, A.W. Tillinghast was called in to construct 36 holes. The Open returned in 1936 and was played on the Upper course. It was won in that year by a surprise champion, Tony Manero, who produced a final round of 67; his total of 282 broke the record aggregate which had stood since 1916. The same year saw the first Open appearance of Ben Hogan: he made no headlines, missing the 36-hole cut.

The US Open was first played on the Lower course in 1954. It was won by Ed Furgol, who had a withered left arm and gave the appearance of hitting with just his right side. In the trees on the final hole, Furgol managed to play out onto the Upper course; as this was not out of bounds, he was able to come through with a par 5. Another player, Dick Mayer, took 8 on the hole: a par would have made him the champion.

In 1967, it was at Baltusrol that Jack Nicklaus won his second US Open. His finish on the 543-yard (497-m) 18th was unusual. He hit off fairly poorly with an iron, played a pitching club short of the creek, and then hammered a magnificent 1-iron to within 6-7 yards (5.5-6.5 m) and holed the putt for an unconventional birdie and a course record 65. He had begun the day level with Arnold Palmer, who had faltered not one bit but whose 69 nevertheless left him four strokes behind Nicklaus.

The 1980 championship was another famous occasion. By this time, Jack Nicklaus's career was very much on the wane. Since 1975 he had won only a single major championship – the 1978 British Open – and in 1979 he had slumped to 71st on the US prize-money list.

TOP Looking back towards Baltusrol's clubhouse from the 4th green. (© TONY ROBERTS 1979)

LEFT The 1st at Baltusrol Lower is a 478-yard (437-m) par 5. (© TONY ROBERTS 1979)

ABOVE Jerry Travers won the second US Open held on the original 9-hole course at Baltusrol in 1915.

1980, despite many lessons on the short game from Phil Rodgers, had likewise not gone well for him. However, in good conditions for scoring and with fast but very holding greens, Nicklaus began with a round of 63, which equalled the lowest round ever shot in the US Open (by Johnny Miller in 1973). Amazingly, it did not give him the outright lead! Tom Weiskopf was already in with the same score. Weiskopf quickly faded away and Nicklaus certainly faltered, being caught by Isao Aoki after the third round, but he carried on both to win the Open and to beat the US Open scoring record with his 272.

Although Jack Nicklaus has twice set US Open scoring records over Baltusrol Lower, this does not mean that the course is easy; rather that it is fair. The greens are neither vast nor small and the contours are gentle. Fairways are relatively wide and bend only gently.

One of the most famous Baltusrol holes is the 4th, a par 3 of nearly 200 yards (180 m), almost all of which is carry over a lake to the green. The green is faced by a stone wall, so there is no chance of a shot that is 'nearly good enough' clambering onto the green. The hole was redesigned by Robert Trent Jones before the 1954 Open and was initially disliked by some of the club's members, who thought it too difficult. Jones went out for a round of golf and holed it in one. No further comment was really necessary!

The course has a great deal of variety; for example, the par 4s are anywhere up to near-maximum length, yet there are five under 400 yards (365 m). The last two holes, however, may between them set a distance record. Two par 5s, they total well over 1,100 yards (1,000 m), a long way to walk if you start off tiredly thinking there are just two holes left to play! The 17th is a monster, at 630 yards (576 m), and is said to be the longest hole ever used in the US Open. It is heavily bunkered, with a patchwork of sandtraps (nicknamed the 'Sahara Desert') at 375 yards (343 m) forming a barrier for some second shots. There is more of the same just short of the green. Nicklaus was ecstatic when he birdied the hole in his 1980 victory: he knew the championship was as good as in his pocket. The last hole is a much shorter par 5, but that statement is relative: it is still over 540 yards (495 m).

BANFF

BANFF SPRINGS HOTEL

BANFF, ALBERTA

CANADA

RIGHT The vast Banff Springs Hotel, itself dominated by its spectacular setting in the Rocky Mountains, looms above the 9th green. (© TONY ROBERTS 1979)

BELOW Another view of the hotel, with the clubhouse and 1st tee in the foreground.

BELOW FAR RIGHT An aerial view of the 1st (left), 18th (right) and the 2nd (left foreground). The 17th green can also be seen (right foreground).

This may not be a great championship test, but it is one of the great places to be, some 4,000 feet (1,220 m) up in the Rockies. The fact that it is too remote for tournament play is one of its strongest attractions.

The course was originally owned by the Canadian Pacific Railway. Nine holes were built before World War I, and more added during that war, German PoWs providing the labour. Several years later, when improvements in equipment made dramatic changes to the landscape more possible, Stanley Thompson redesigned Banff. There was much quarrying, blasting and removal of tree stumps; he also increased the bunkering. Today, there are about 150 bunkers, at least 25 of these being on the 18th!

There is no doubt at all which is the most famous hole on the course. This is the 8th, also known as 'The Devil's Cauldron'; it is one of the most scenic in the world. It is a par 3 of 175

yards (160 m), played from a high tee to a green set close up to the fringe of a pine forest, with the Rockies rearing up behind. But those are not all of the spectacular features of the hole. Between the tee and the dropping shot to the green lies an expanse of water. The hole plays relatively short and so it looks more testing than it actually is; even so, poorer golfers can find themselves running out of golf balls.

The start of the course requires a tee shot over the Spray River; no great carry is needed. It is the Bow River which is the main feature of the course. It provides a threat to the right of holes 12 to 18, with Thompson's bunkering being often heavy along the left. The 14th is a very demanding par 3 of more than 200 yards (180 m). The tee shot is over water, with the ground in the landing area sloping towards this pond. Perhaps the most interesting hole, however, is the 7th, a par 5 of just over 500 yards (460 m) which can in the thin mountain air be reached in two — but it is a perilous task, with the precipitous slopes of Mount Rundle to the right, bunkers along the left, and a sharp dogleg leading to the green.

THE COUNTRY CLUB

BELOW Vast bunkers threaten the narrow entrance to this Brookline green. (© LEONARD KAMSLER 1987)

The very name sounds arrogant, but this was the first club of the type in the United States (1860), so the choice was natural. Golf did not arrive until about 1890, however, when the club's committee made provision in the annual budget for $50 to be spent on the preparation of a nine-hole course. Four years later, The Country Club was one of the five founder members of the United States Golf Association. By 1909, golf had caught on in the Boston area to the extent that a further nine holes were added. By then the annual match against Royal Montreal Golf Club had become almost a part of The Country Club's traditions; this match, first held in 1898, was the earliest international golf match.

The Country Club's greatest fame dates, however, from 1913. Only two US Opens have been held on the course, but the 1913 Open was one of the greatest and was also, in its way, an international match. It almost saw the emergence of

Walter Hagen, who came in fourth. Ahead of him, tied for first place were Henry Vardon and Ted Ray, of England, and Francis de Sales Ouimet of the United States. Vardon had won the 1900 US Open and the British Open five times (he was to win it a sixth time in 1914). Ted Ray had won the 1912 British Open. Ouimet, by contrast, was a 20-year-old US amateur who in four attempts had only once qualified to play the US Amateur event and who was having great difficulty at the time in breaking the 90 barrier. He entered the competition solely because the Open was being played at his home town!

After three rounds, Ouimet was level with Vardon and Ray, but then apparently threw his chances away with 43 to the turn quickly followed by a 5 on the 10th (then a par 3). Yet he managed to play the last six holes in two under par to tie. No one thought it mattered much. He had had a very good day and deserved full credit.

BELOW The protagonists in the greatest upset in the history of golf – Harry Vardon (left), Francis Ouimet (middle) and Ted Ray. Here they are pictured on the morning of the 18-hole play-off for the 1913 US Open.

But the general attitude was: who would win the 18-hole play-off, Vardon or Ray?

Each of the three took 38 strokes for the first nine, but at the 10th Ouimet took the lead. He finally made the championship his with a birdie 3 on the 17th, where Vardon took 5. The final scores make it look even easier for Ouimet: he was round in 72, to Vardon's 77 and Ray's 78. Although Ouimet was not the first US-born winner (that was Johnny McDermott in 1911), he was the first to beat Vardon and his is still the outstanding rags-to-riches story in terms of a major golfing championship. His victory greatly increased interest in golf in the United States, especially on the sports pages, where golf had tended to be treated as a pastime of the rich rather than as a popular sport.

The US Open returned to The Country Club in 1963 to commemorate the 50th anniversary of Ouimet's feat. During Ouimet's victory, the course had been waterlogged, and for Julius Boros's second Open win (he had previously won in 1952) the weather was just as bad – perhaps not as wet, but colder. His 293 is by 3 strokes the highest winning score in the US Open since World War II, mostly because of the conditions rather than any innate difficulty of the course.

Brookline, at first view, looks like a mere parkland walk, the 18 holes used for the Open being made up of a selection from the club's 27. The start, however, is stiff: between a couple of long par 4s is a 190-yard (175-m) par 3. The other six of the first nine present less of a challenge, although the 500-yard (460-m) 9th offers the chance of playing short of a stony rise or going for the carry.

Thereafter, the course retains its parkland character, but it is much narrower. The 10th, 11th and 12th are all long 4s; the 12th is especially so, almost par-5 distance, with the long second shot inevitably finding a greenside bunker unless it is perfectly judged in terms of both strength and direction. The last three holes are strangely short for a championship course, a par 3 needing no more than a medium iron followed by two drive-and-pitch holes to complete the round. However, as we saw, Vardon foundered on the 17th in 1913, and he has been far from alone. In the 1963 Open Jackie Cupit would have won outright had he been able to complete the last two holes two over par: he took 6 and Arnold Palmer 5, to tie with Julius Boros. (Tony Lema, who had been in contention, like Palmer took 5.) Boros, who had single-putted the 17th, went on to win the play-off the following day. Clearly any hole which can so dramatically affect the result of major championships is not as innocuous as it looks!

CYPRESS POINT

Although undeniably one of the world's very greatest courses, Cypress Point is under 6,500 yards (5,950 m) long. With Merion, which is of a similar length, it constitutes one of the best arguments in golf that a course does not have to be 7,000 yards (6,400 m) long to be fit to host a championship. In fact, Cypress Point is much more of a test than most of the 'monsters'.

It does have two weaknesses. Everyone agrees that the last hole is little more than a shortcut back to the clubhouse, a drive-and-pitch hole with usually only the top of the flag in view for the second shot. The 16th is more controversial, and is probably the most photographed hole in golf. It is 233 yards (213 m) long and requires a drive with a carry of about 210 yards (190 m) to cross a Pacific inlet to the green, which is set on a headland. The irony is that Dr Alister Mackenzie, who designed the course in the 1920s, is thought to have planned the hole quite differently: he made it as a par 4, with the tee set further back and needing a drive of only moderate carry. The second shot was to be from the area of fairway that modern players who cannot hope to make the 210-yard (190-m) carry play for. As it is today, however, the 16th demands just about the most heroic shot in the game – but is it golf? Even so, there have been holes in one here – Bing Crosby was the second to do it.

The holes either side of the 16th are more strategic. The 15th does need a direct carry over a rocky inlet to the green but, since the distance is only 130 yards (120 m) or so, the bunkers that follow the inlet are more of a threat. The 17th, at 375 yards (343 m), is a magnificent par 4. The drive is from a high tee up in the cliffs, with the Pacific on the right. The golfer has to decide exactly which angle to attempt as the cliffs bite in.

These are the holes providing the highest drama, set at the very tip of the Monterey Peninsula, but all of Cypress Point gives the player very good golf. The 1st is played down to a valley curving to the right, and at 420 yards (384 m) is a severe enough start. The 2nd, nearly 550 yards (500 m) in length, is the longest hole on the course and has a demanding tee shot requiring a diagonal carry. There are trees along the right and dunes to the left, and the green is

CYPRESS POINT
GOLF CLUB
PEBBLE BEACH
CALIFORNIA
UNITED STATES

RIGHT AND FAR RIGHT The most photographed hole in golf is the 16th (far right) at Cypress Point with its frightening carry over the sea. There is less to fear at the 15th (right), which is also a par 3 and scenically every bit as spectacular.

heavily bunkered.

After the 2nd the course heads for a wooded hillside, the setting of the 5th through to the 11th. The 7th is a par 3 of 160 yards (146 m) played from one hill to another over a valley, and the 9th shows that even a downhill par 4 of just 290 yards (265 m) can be difficult; its small hard green can be very tricky to hold.

The 5th and 10th greens are at the farthest points of the course. At the 11th tee the golfer heads back towards the rocky peninsula, with the 13th and 14th being seaside holes before the clifftops are reached.

Cypress Point is manifestly a course of championship standard: it is one of the best in the world. However, no championships have been held on it, although Bing Crosby moved his tournament to the peninsula from Rancho Santa Fe after World War II. Since then Pebble Beach and Cypress Point have been used for the tournament each year – as, since 1966, has Spyglass Hill.

Ironically for such a highly respected course, Cypress Hill breaks a few of the 'rules' of golf-course design. It has two par 5s in a row (the 5th and 6th), and indeed all four of the par 5s come between the 2nd and 10th. Similarly, two par 3s (the 15th and 16th) are back to back. No one, however, complains of anything at Cypress Point – except the 18th, and that may partly be simply a product of the contrast with the glories just experienced.

Many superlatives have been used about the course. One reverential comment was that Cypress Point is the Sistine Chapel of golf; while a newspaperman once said that it was the dream of 'an artist who had been drinking gin and sobering up on absinthe'. It is unlikely that there is a better-looking course in the world.

DURBAN

Carved out of bush and through sand dunes in the early 1920s, this is South Africa's finest course and plays host to most major events held in Natal. The original architect was Laurie Waters, in 1920. His course has remained basically little changed although many later architects, including S. V. Hotchkin from Woodhall Spa, England, and Bob Grimsdell, late in the 1950s, have had a hand in it. By that time, the main aim was to cope with the modern ball and increase the course's length to nearly 6,600 yards (6,035 m). Even so, this distance is still a little short by modern standards, mainly because the par 3s are reasonable in length and there are a number of drive-and-pitch par 4s.

Durban is a popular venue for the South African Open. Indeed, it was thanks to this event that the course was created in the first place: the

Royal Durban course became hopelessly waterlogged during the 1919 national championship, and it was felt that the city needed a more reliable alternative. Since that time, many Open Championships have been held here. Among the Durban champions have been Bobby Locke, Gary Player, Bob Charles and Bobby Cole (in 1980 doing something to justify his earlier promise). Gary Player won his first Open here in 1956 and over 20 years later overhauled Bobby Locke's record when he won his 10th championship.

Another famous achievement on the course belongs to the Duke of Windsor (Edward VIII). When, as Prince of Wales, this keen golfer played the 12th, a shortish par 3 of under 150 yards (137 m), he needed no fewer than 17 strokes to hole out; the green is raised and the future king went down a bank to the right, returning only after some little while! Among the course's four par 3s, however, the 180-yard (165 m) 2nd normally gives more trouble. It is played from a high tee to a raised green, surrounded by bunkers and scrub, with a valley in between.

The 3rd is the most famous hole on the course. This again has an elevated tee shot down into a valley. The ground then rises to the green, humpy all the way with scrub and trees on either side. Only just over 500 yards (460 m) long, the 3rd offers the prospect of getting home in two – but both shots must be long and placed with absolute precision.

The majority of the middle holes of the course are played on flat land, but the finish is among dunes and close to the Indian Ocean. The 16th, a little under 400 yards (365 m) in length, plays long because there is a climb to the green which is set up among the dunes. The 17th has as tumbling a fairway as you could find. The 18th, only 276 yards (252 m) long, seems superficially hardly a testing finishing hole. It is indeed drivable, but the ground falls away steeply to the right and there are bushes along the left. The temptation of going for the green with a big drive causes many golfers to come unstuck. However, the 1928 South African champion, Jock Brews, finished in style: he drove the green, holed the putt, and won by a stroke.

ABOVE Bobby Locke won nine South African Open Championships, a record surpassed by only Gary Player.

LEFT The approach to the 18th green with the clubhouse in the background.

FAR LEFT TOP An aerial view of the Durban Country Club complex with the 18th green to the right of the clubhouse.

FAR LEFT BOTTOM This panoramic view reveals the humps and hollows of the course which was carved out of sand dunes and bush. The 1st, 2nd, 17th and 18th holes and the 16th green, surrounded by three bunkers, are on view.

GLENEAGLES KING'S COURSE

GLENEAGLES HOTEL

AUCHTERARDER

PERTHSHIRE

SCOTLAND

BELOW The famous hotel at Gleneagles, completed in the early 1920s.

When James Braid was asked before World War I to design two courses for Gleneagles, his brief was a testing one. Building courses of stunning difficulty presents its fair share of construction problems, but Braid was required to produce golf courses that holiday-makers would find enjoyable. He designed the King's Course (18 holes) and the Queen's (only nine holes at first). In the years since then Gleneagles has grown to become a golf complex with four courses, the King's, Queen's, Prince's and Glendevon. Of these, the King's supplies the sternest test, mainly because it is easily the longest. The Queen's is the most beautiful of the four. All, however, benefit from their exquisite natural surroundings: the Ochil Hills, the Grampian Mountains and the Trossachs, all seen from a moorland setting some 500 feet (150 m) above sea-level.

The 1st hole of the King's offers an inviting start, a par 4 of 360 yards (330 m) with a wide fairway, the ground rising to the green, which is on the skyline. Although the line in to the green is barred by a cross bunker, this should cause little difficulty as most golfers will have only a pitch to play from the fairway. However, the green itself causes problems with its back-to-front slope. This presents more difficulties to players of professional standard than to ordinary club players: the professionals find their shots can spin back and off the green. At over 400 yards (335 m), the 2nd might seem more of a challenge, but it is played downhill and the only real difficulty is that the fairway is narrow with, as is usual at Gleneagles, gorse, bracken and heather on both flanks. The 3rd, uphill, needs an iron shot carrying all the way to the correct level of the two-tier green. Most people agree that the

ABOVE Of the Great Triumvirate – Vardon, Braid and Taylor – only Braid went on to become a leading figure in golf course design. Here he is pictured near the beginning of this century after winning the first of his five British Opens in 1901.

5th is the best of the par 3s. It has a little of the appearance of an Iron Age fort, with the ground falling away all around; it is set with large deep bunkers.

The finish, however, betrays the fact that the course was never intended as a championship test. The 14th, although a par 4, is played as a par 3 by strong hitters, the main problem arising if the flag is set to the front of the green – the shot in can readily run to the back. The 15th is more formidable in length, at 460 yards (421m), but the second shot is downhill and so the hole does not play long. The 16th is quite a short par 3; but the 17th has the tightest tee shot on the course and is followed by an approach to a plateau green which you have to judge carefully. A par 5 at the finish of any course should always be relatively easy, and the 18th on the King's is welcoming indeed. 525 yards (480 m) in length, it is played from a high tee and the green is one of the biggest targets in golf. Tom Watson once had a measured drive of 486 yards (444 m) here, helped by the run of the ground and a following wind. Average club players will find an intervening rise more difficult to carry, but rich rewards follow.

Although the Gleneagles Hotel did not open until the mid-1920s, the King's Course was ready to play in 1919, and two years later the first match between the United States and a combined British and Irish team was played here, the US team being trounced. A professional tournament was played here in the 1930s, as well as the 1936 Curtis Cup, but the courses were mainly reserved for holiday golf, a facility of the vast luxury hotel.

In 1987, however, the Scottish Open was played at Gleneagles. There was some remarkable scoring. The Spanish golfer Jose-Maria Olazabal set a new course record over the 6,800 yards (6,218 m) of the King's Course, with a 62, and Ian Woosnam, in a dominating performance, opened up with a pair of 65s and was 20 under par when he won by 7 strokes. The weather created no problems and the greens were both holding and superbly true for putting, a recipe for low scoring, but even so the lengthened course proved that it would yield only to very good play. Many felt that Woosnam might well go on to win the British Open Championship the following week, so well was he striking the ball and putting. Instead, it went to another British player, Nick Faldo, who won from a likely future star, Paul Azinger.

HARBOUR TOWN

Pete Dye already had a reputation as a golf architect before he created Harbour Town, but this course made him a celebrity. There was almost instant exposure of his work, with Arnold Palmer winning the Heritage Classic here only a few weeks after the course opened, in 1969. The name of this US Tour event pays tribute to the United States' golfing past, which goes back at least as far as 1779 (and possibly over a century earlier). The South Carolina Golf Club, the first in the United States, was founded in Charleston in 1786. This great antiquity of the game in South Carolina is paralleled by Dye's interest in traditional golf achitecture, which manifests itself in a liking for undulations in the ground, liberal bunkering and the use of heavy timber shoring for bunkers and greens. At Harbour Town, however, Dye was hardly able to indulge his liking for undulations: the highest point of the course is no more than a few feet above the lowest. The main hazards are water features, which have a profound effect on most of the holes. Although there are no great unavoidable carries to be made on the longer holes, the par 3s tend to be frighteners. The first of these is the 4th, about 180 yards (165 m) long, where the green pushes out into the water on one side and is shorn up by timbers. The 7th is a little shorter, under 170 yards (155 m); although there is again a water carry, the main hazard comes immediately afterward: a large sandy area. The 14th, at 150 yards (137 m), is carry all the way, and also has a creek circling the green to the right. And the last of the par 3s, the 190-yard (174-m) 17th, is highly unusual. Although a creek runs all along the left of the green, it is separated from the green itself by a long bunker, with a retaining wall of timber. The position of the tee was changed here early on because tournament professionals protested that they could not hold the green.

The 17th is followed by the most severe hole on the course, a par 4 of near maximum length. Two big shots are needed to clear the encroaching tidal salt marsh of Calibogue Sound, the drive being to what is in effect an island fairway. Played this way, the hole is virtually dead straight, but the power of shot needed is beyond the capacity of most golfers. The alternative is to play right of the marshes. This approach puts

the green out of reach in 2, but renders the hole a relatively easy 5.

As well as the water, trees provide a major hazard on a course which is generally pleasant rather than frightening to play. Aside from those carries to the par 3s, water is used mostly as a feature to the sides of greens and fairways. Trees serve to define and narrow the landing area for tee shots. The course, at less than 6,700 yards (6,125 m), is short for a modern tournament course. Although the professionals have produced some very low scores during the Heritage, it is recognized that only the very best are ever likely to win here. Yet there are several par 4s of only drive-and-pitch distance. The 9th, at only just over 320 yards (295 m), is the shortest of these and is indeed drivable for some — the only snag being the large bunker that blocks the line into the green. The 13th proves that a par 4 does not need to be long to be good: it is just over 350 yards (320 m), but the narrow fairway must be hit precisely, because the encroaching trees make the line in to the green — which is slightly elevated and surrounded by sand, except to the rear — extremely tight.

Although bunkers of often extravagant shapes are a notable sight at Harbour Town, there are only about 50 of them in all, and not a few are placed to define the target areas rather than to trap balls. This represents an intelligent approach to golf architecture, especially on flat land.

ABOVE A typically extravagant design feature of Harbour Town are the vast swathes of sand encircling the green. This is the 165-yard (150-m) 7th hole.

LEFT With the 9th green in the foreground, this scene epitomizes the period charm of South Carolina.

RIGHT There is more than golf at Harbour Town as can be seen in this view of the yacht basin and the 18th green.

INVERNESS CLUB
TOLEDO, OHIO
UNITED STATES

RIGHT The clubhouse and 18th green during the 1986 PGA Championship.

FAR RIGHT The scoreboard tells the full story of Greg Norman's slump during the final round of the 1986 PGA Championship.

INVERNESS

One reason for the fame of Inverness is the way that two of its holes have been played 'the wrong way' to great effect.

First came Ted Ray in the 1920 US Open, playing the 7th, which was then a doglegged par 4 of 334 yards (305 m) with trees and a deep pit at the angle. A prodigious hitter, perhaps, could carry the lot and finish on the green. Ted Ray, one of the most violent of men in his dealings with a golf ball, threw everything into the shot in all four rounds. Each time he was successful in making the carry of some 270 yards (250 m); each time he came out with a birdie 3. As he won the Open by just one stroke from a cluster of players – Harry Vardon, Jock Hutchison, Jack Burke and Leo Diegel – it could be claimed that his scoring on the 7th won the last US Open to go to a UK player until Tony Jacklin did it exactly 50 years later, in 1970.

The other hole to have been played 'the wrong way' is the 8th. Before the 1979 US Open at Inverness, architect George Fazio made four new holes. One that disappeared was the historic 7th, which was used as part of one of the new holes, the 8th, a par 5 of 528 yards (483 m). But Fazio slipped up: he failed to realize that players could drive through a gap in the trees onto the 17th fairway and so make the hole easier. After a few players had done this in the first round, the USGA planted a 25-foot (7.6-m) spruce tree overnight to close the gap. However, the tree was not tall enough, and some players continued to play up the 17th. Today the gap is filled by a generous clump of trees!

The Inverness Club was founded in 1903 and named for the castle in Scotland where in 1040 Macbeth had King Duncan murdered. Nine holes were planned for a start, but the first architect to work at Inverness had a problem with his arithmetic. As he stood back to admire his handiwork it was suddenly realized that there were in fact only eight holes. Very embarrassing! However, Bernard Nicholls hurriedly tacked on a par 3, which in the event proved to be a very good hole.

Other architects have been involved in the development of the course. A year before Ted Ray's Open triumph, Donald Ross designed a second nine; A W Tillinghast made revisions a

few years later for the 1931 Open; and Dick Wilson did likewise for the 1957 Open. And then, as we have seen, came Fazio.

All Inverness's four US Opens to date have been remarkable in some way, sometimes with elements of the absurd. Take 1931, the first after the retirement of Bobby Jones. Billy Burke and George Von Elm tied. The play-off in those days was over 36 holes – but not that year. After the day's play they were still tied, so out they had to go the following morning to do it all again. Burke came through, but only by a single stroke after the 144 holes of golf, making the 1931 US Open the longest major championship of all time.

In 1957, Jimmy Demaret thought he had the championship in the bag, but then Dick Mayer

	HOLE	1	2	3	4	5	6	7	8	9	10	11	12	13	14	15	16	17	18
LEADERS	PAR	4	4	3	4	4	3	4	5	4	4	4	3	5	4	4	4	4	4
11	NORMAN	11	11	10	10	10	9		9	10	8	8							
7	TWAY	7	7	8	8	8	7	7	6	6	6	7							
5	JACOBSEN	4	4	4	5	5	5	4	4	4	4	4							
4	HAMMOND	3	2	3	2	2	2	2	2	2	2	3	3						
4	STEWART	4	4	4	3	3	3	3	3	2	2	2	2						
3	LIETZKE	2	2	2	3	3	3	2	3	2	2	2	2						
2	THORPE	1	1	1	1	1	0	1	2	2	1	0							
2	WEIBRING	1	1	2	3	2	3	2	2	2	2								
3	NICKLAUS	2	3	3	2	1	1	1	1	0	1								
2	HULBERT	1	1	1	2	1	1	0	0	1	0								

ABOVE In the 1986 PGA Norman and Bob Tway went into the last hole level. Tway holed out for a 3 from a greenside bunker and was suddenly champion.

holed a birdie putt of nearly 20 feet (6 m) to edge ahead, in due course tying with Cary Middlecoff, who was able to birdie the same hole during his second 68 of the day, a remarkable finish. Middlecoff was one of the first of modern golf's really slow players, taking an age to align and set himself up for a shot. Mayer thought there was a point to be made. He took out a camping stool for the 18-hole play-off. Perhaps the success of the psychological ploy was more important than Mayer's comfort while he waited for Middlecoff to play his shots. The result was: Mayer 72, Middlecoff 79.

Hale Irwin, neither a very long hitter nor an outstanding putter, has often performed best on the more difficult courses. Difficult Inverness most certainly is. The greens are much smaller than average, and they are as subtly contoured and frighteningly fast as any. It is vital to place the tee shot perfectly to give a good line in and to land the shot to the green below the hole (with a downhill putt, the player has to think mainly about how he or she can stop the ball running well past the hole).

In the 1979 US Open Irwin managed this very well so that, with nine holes to play, he was a full 6 strokes ahead of anyone else in the field. Then he began to come apart. The problem was his tee shots: he hit a succession of them into the rough to the left or right, behind trees and into bunkers. He finished his round with a double bogey and a bogey. However, he had still managed to preserve enough of his lead to win by a couple of strokes.

JAGORAWI

JAGORAWI GOLF AND
COUNTRY CLUB
CIBINONG
INDONESIA

Approached by a 35-mile (56-km) dirt road from Jakarta, Jagorawi is a course that was cut through jungle; as a result, it has the 'feel' of being entirely divorced from the outside world. Each hole is almost a tropical garden in its own right, and great attention has been paid to detail: witness the stonework and timber revetment on some of the bunkers. Water comes strongly into play on half of the holes, sometimes as a barrier for the tee shots and elsewhere for shots to the greens.

Architect Ronald Fream had the aims of beauty and tranquillity, as well as the provision of a good test of golf. He learned his trade with Robert Trent Jones before working with the Thomson and Woolveridge partnership and then becoming independent.

There are five par 5s which challenge a brave line of shot. The 1st is a memorable hole, with a tee set high above the fairway and a carry to be made over the Cisadene River; as the hole is set in a U-bend of the river, water continues in play up either side of the narrowing fairway. The 9th, doglegging right, tempts longer hitters to cut across the angle, although a well placed bunker catches many.

The choice is much the same on the 15th, a banana-shaped hole where the golfer has the option of playing either for safety or for the glory of being home in two; because the paddy fields along the right were owned in penny packets, there were continuous delays in negotiating the sales to the club, and the architect eventually settled on the extreme left-to-right shape of the final design.

Besides the Cisadene River, there is a tributary stream that forms a hazard running through the middle of the course. Often the stream has to be carried for a shot through the green, while at other times it is in play for shots that stray to the left or right.

Jagorawi was opened towards the end of the 1970s and the tropical climate means that it already has a mature appearance. A second course, intended to be public, is at the planning stage. The great tournaments may never come to Jagorawi but, when dusk comes suddenly, this is one of the most beautiful places in the world for a golfer to be.

LEFT The course at Jagorawi was cut through the tropical jungle. Here is the 10th with the 11th green in the background.

MEDINAH NUMBER 3

MEDINAH COUNTRY
CLUB, MEDINAH
ILLINOIS
UNITED STATES

RIGHT A view of the 17th
(to the left) and 18th
greens. The par-3 17th
requires a carry over
Lake Kadijah. (© TONY
ROBERTS 1986)

One man more than any other has come to be reviled in the history of golf architecture – Tom Bendelow. He was a Scot who came to the United States to work as a printer for a New York newspaper and, by the mid-1890s, found himself working for Spaldings as a golf-course architect. How did this happen? We can only speculate, but it was probably because of Scotland's reputation as the home of golf: anyone from that country should be able to design a course in an afternoon! Which is precisely what Tom Bendelow often did. Arming himself with a bundle of stakes, he knocked one in for a tee. Then he walked forward a hundred yards or two and banged in the next stake to indicate that a cross bunker should be dug. After choosing the site for his green, he put in his fourth stake to mark it (the third stake was already in to show where a bunker should be dug or some humps built up short of the green). Tom then left instructions as to how the course should be built and maintained, took the cheque – usually $25 – and was on his way.

Actually, Tom was no worse than anyone else: that was the way golf architecture was in the United States in the 1890s – and it was little better in the UK. He improved with time, gave the subject far more thought, and in due course even lectured about it at the University of Illinois. He is still given credit for Medinah Number 3, which is absurd as he set it out as a course specifically designed for women and it has been totally transformed over the years since then.

Today, Medinah is a formidable course indeed. The whole complex was originally built for members of the Ancient Arabic Order of Nobles of the Mystic Shrine. Appropriately, the clubhouse is Moslem in inspiration, little expense being spared in its construction during the free-spending 1920s, when the club included also provision for skiing and polo.

The Medinah Number 3 course has been used for two US Opens, those of 1949 and 1975. They were won, respectively, by Cary Middlecoff, a qualified dentist turned golfer, and Lou Graham. Both matches turned on the last holes.

In 1949 the central characters in the drama were Middlecoff, the late great Clayton Heafner – the angriest man ever to play golf! – and Sam

Snead. Heafner dropped a shot on the 17th and missed a shortish putt on the last. Snead tried to run a putt through the fringe around the 17th instead of lofting his ball over, and failed. Both finished a stroke behind Middlecoff. With Ben Hogan not in the field, following his famous car smash, these were just about the best players in the field.

It was all rather different the next time the US Open came to Medinah, in 1975. This time, the two contenders at the end had somewhat less charisma. They were John Mahaffey and Lou Graham. They tied, with Mahaffey, unable to hole a putt, losing the 18-hole play-off – the last (to end 1987) required in the US Open. The 1975 championship, however, is probably more notable for the collapse of a future great player. After two rounds, Tom Watson was three strokes in the lead and his start of 67 and 68 had tied the

US Open record. His finish of 78, 77 was dismal, to put it mildly, and gave rise to much talk about his lack of nerve. The following month, as an unknown in Great Britain, he confounded his critics by winning the Open Championship.

Medinah Number 3 can often feel a claustrophobic course, trees seeming to cramp you on almost all of the holes. Lake Kadijah is the main feature, although it is in play on at most three holes. The first occasion is at the 2nd, a par 3 of around 190 yards (175 m) played over the lake; the next tee shot is played over a finger of water but no carry from the tee is needed. By this time, golfers are well into heavily wooded country. Soon they come to the first of the three par 5s. This one, the 5th, is no 'monster' – at about 530 yards (485 m) – and provides a birdie opportunity for tournament players. The 7th, however, is brutal: close to 600 yards (550 m), and with a dogleg, it has a very heavily bunkered green.

The 13th, however, is the most difficult hole on the course. Over 450 yards (410 m) long, it doglegs sharply left around the woods. Only a precisely placed drive gives any real chance of getting home in two with anything other than a wood or a long iron.

But the hole that has decided championships is the 17th, a par 3 of around 220 yards (200 m) which starts off requiring a carry over Lake Kadijah, followed by one over a bank set with a deep bunker. The shot to the green requires absolute precision: there are no alternative routes. Here, in 1975, the young Ben Crenshaw, then heir-apparent to Jack Nicklaus, hit a 2-iron a little towards the toe of the club and took 5: he may never win the US Open which, because of Medinah's 17th, so narrowly slipped from his grasp way back at the beginning of his career.

ABOVE The trees crowd around the 2nd green at Medinah No 3. A par-3 hole of 190 yards (175 m), it must be played over the main feature of the course, Lake Kadijah. (© TONY ROBERTS 1986)

MERION EAST

MERION GOLF CLUB
ARDMORE
PHILADELPHIA
PENNSYLVANIA
UNITED STATES

ABOVE Hugh Wilson was a complete amateur in golf architecture, but produced one of the United States' greatest courses at Merion.

The Merion club dates back to Civil War times, but one should not think that golf arrived here particularly early. Cricket was more the thing for Philadelphians at that time. They even sent touring sides to England during the 19th century: these proved to have some very fine players and gave promise that the United States could well become a leading cricketing nation; despite Philadelphia's John King topping the English first-class bowling averages in 1908, this dream was never to be realized.

Anyhow, Merion Cricket Club it was for many years, the adjective not being changed in favour of 'Golf' until 1942. By then, however, golf had long been established, and had been the main activity of the club since about 1900.

The first course, with nine holes, was opened in the mid-1890s, and a farther nine were added a few years later. In 1904 and 1909, the US Women's Championship was played over it. For men, however, the arrival of the rubber-core ball around the turn of the century was making virtually all courses too short. The members of Merion wanted a championship lay-out. They formed a committee to consider the matter and one member of it, Hugh Wilson, showed such a grasp of golf architecture that he was asked to do the job. Like Charles Blair Macdonald in the matter of the National Golf Links, he decided to make a pilgrimage to Britain. Beforehand, he asked Macdonald which courses were the best for him to inspect. He was away from the United States seven months, and he returned with many notes and drawings of what had impressed him.

The 127 acres (51 ha) he had to work with is near the minimum for a championship lay-out, and the land itself was hardly promising: thin layers of clay soil over rock. The ground was undulating (some might say bumpy) but it did have some natural features that he could put to good use — two brooks and a disused stone quarry. In fact, he put them to such good use that some people consider Merion East the finest course in the United States. Two of its holes, the 1st and the 11th, are listed in Dan Jenkins' book *The Best Eighteen Golf Holes in America*: no other course has more than one hole honoured.

In 1914, the US Amateur Championship came to Merion and saw the first major appearance of a man who was to have associations with the course throughout his career. That man was Robert Tyre Jones Jr, who arrived in 1914 as a 14-year-old who already had a local reputation down in his native Atlanta. Bobby Jones, playing on the West Course, also designed by Hugh Wilson, started off with a 74 — phenomenal scoring in those days. The spotlights were concentrated on him for the second qualifying round and he subsided to an 89, but this was still good enough for him to qualify and go on to beat a former amateur champion in the first round before going out to the defending champion, Bob Gardner, later.

In 1924, Jones won the first of his five US Amateur Championships at Merion and it was here that, six years later, he won his last: with this victory, he completed the almost impossible feat of winning the British and US Open and Amateur Championships in the same year (1930). That Merion win was his last: Jones felt he had done it all and retired, 13 major championships to his credit. No one has equalled his five US Amateur titles while, of current players, it took Jack Nicklaus until 1980 to match Jones's four US Open titles, a feat earlier accomplished only by Willie Anderson and Ben Hogan.

The US Open first came to Merion in 1934. Coming from eight strokes behind after 36 holes, there was a new champion, Olin Dutra. His total of 293 says something for the difficulty of the course. Sixteen years later, Ben Hogan tied for the championship with 287, one of the highest scores since World War II, and won the play-off. This was one of his most impressive victories because he had been left for dead in a car smash early in 1949 and had been out of golf for nearly a year. Even by the time of the 1950 Open in June, although most conceded that Hogan was the best man in the field, just as many doubted that his legs would carry him for the 36 holes of play on the final day. Hogan managed, although he nearly withdrew with cramp on the second nine of his last round; he then had to go another 18 holes the following day in the play-off.

By 1971, there was a new generation of

RIGHT, Walter Hagen, here pictured late in his career, was an ardent admirer of the course.

BELOW RIGHT In February 1949 Ben Hogan was terribly injured when his car was in collision with a bus. Surely he would never play golf again? Here he is winning the 1950 US Open at Merion.

BELOW LEFT Bobby Jones retired shortly after winning his last major championship at Merion. This was the 1930 US Amateur which gave him the Grand Slam of the then four major titles – the US and British Amateur and Open Championships.

golfers, and no one doubted that the two out-standing players were Lee Trevino and Jack Nicklaus. It was entirely fitting that they should tie for the title, which Trevino won in the play-off over 18 holes. Their 280 for 72 holes was even par.

In 1981, however, par was beaten, this time by five players, David Graham's total being 273. His last round 67, in which he hit nearly every fair-way and all the greens in regulation figures, is reckoned the equal of any round of golf ever played.

The scores given here say something of the difficulties of Merion (Masters champion George Archer once declared that 95 per cent of the US Open field of 1971 were just not good enough to play it!). Yet it is no monster. Its length, 6,544 yards (5,984 m), is a good 300 yards (275 m) shorter than is otherwise used for any major championship, and almost the same comment applies to any tournament played on either the US or European Tours. Surely a winner ought to come home with an average of 66, but this has never seemed likely at Merion. Trevino, when he first saw the course, went out and played a few holes and thought that the key was to hit the tee shot into the fairway after which everything would be straightforward enough. A very short while later he was calling Merion the hardest course he had ever seen!

Trevino's judgement – that the best ploy was to make sure to hit the fairway – was right as far as it went: the rough is certainly punishing. But the real key is to find the right part of the fairway so that the shot to the green can be eased. For the same event, Jack Nicklaus planned to use his driver on only three holes; the rest of the time he felt position was far more important than length. The greens must be attacked from the right quarter. They are often small and well defended and, for championship play, they are hard and very, very fast.

Most architects make their 1st hole a gentle introduction. To the unwary this can at first seem to be the case at Merion. Only 355 yards (325 m) long, it is on the face of it certainly just a drive-and-pitch hole, although very well bunkered to either side of the fairway and with a green that slopes both from right to left and, more of a problem, front to rear. Later, there is a spell of four more short par 4s in the space of five holes.

One of these — the 10th — is only 312 yards (285 m) long, and so obviously the big hitters look to drive it. Twice in the 1971 Open Jack Nicklaus was not on in two. The 11th has seen much history. When Jones parred it in 1930 in the final he had won the US Amateur by 8 and 7 and completed his slam. Four years later, Gene Sarazen, leading the US Open, took 7 for

LEFT Although the 10th hole at Merion measures only 312 yards (285 m) it can be fatal to miss the small green as you could find an impossible lie in this bunker.

the hole and went on to lose the champion-ship by a stroke. In the same event, Bobby Cruickshank hit a poor second shot which pitched into Cobb's Creek before the green. His ball struck a rock and bounded up into the air and onto the green. 'Thank you, Lord!' cried Bobby, tossing his club on high. A second or two later, it felled him. Cruickshank lost his championship lead – and his playing partner's concentration disappeared too as he collapsed in laughter.

At the finish, strong hitting is needed. At each of the last three holes the disused quarry is a feature. The 16th, about 430 yards (395 m), needs a second shot that carries all the way to the green; and the 17th, over 220 yards (200 m),

easily the longest of Merion's four par 3s, is over the quarry to a green flanked by bunkers, with a swale reminiscent of the Valley of Sin at St Andrews' 18th. Merion's 18th, about 460 yards (420 m), needs 220 yards (200 m) of carry to reach the fairway, and the second shot is always a long iron. Needing a 4 to tie in 1950, Hogan hit a 1-iron to the green: that historic club was promptly stolen from his golf bag.

Perhaps Walter Hagen made the best sum-mation of Merion. He thought it a fair course where you always believed you would break 70 ... next time. Playing past his prime in 1934 Hagen started with a 76, then got a 69. Had he discovered the secret? Apparently not. He finished with 83 and 80.

ABOVE The clubhouse at Merion has seen the climaxes of many great championships.

MUIRFIELD

THE HONOURABLE
COMPANY OF
EDINBURGH GOLFERS
GULLANE
EAST LOTHIAN
SCOTLAND

BELOW A great par 3, the green at the 13th has some perilously deep bunkers guarding it. Just getting out of one bunker can be a triumph and the player can still find himself in yet another.

Founded by 1774 and responsible in that same year for the first known code of golf rules, the Honourable Company of Edinburgh Golfers is the oldest golfing club or society with a continuous history. These men of Edinburgh first played over Leith Links, but in 1836 they moved to Musselburgh. Use of the course by other clubs led to the move to Muirfield in 1891, the Open Championship going with the club — much to the anger of the men of Musselburgh. Ironically, when the first Muirfield Open was held, in 1892, the course came in for much criticism. One St Andrews competitor called it 'a damned water meadow'. The great golf writer Bernard Darwin thought that it gave 'the impression of an inland park'. And five-times Open Champion J.H. Taylor later wrote that the course was not fit to be the home of such a great club.

Perhaps the main problem was that it was new. Who would think in modern times of playing a championship on a course laid out only a year before, as Muirfield had been (by old Tom Morris)? It was also, even for the days of the guttie ball, rather short: 5,500 yards (5,030 m). One aspect of the design was revolutionary. Almost all courses before Morris's scheme for Muirfield had had an out-and-back layout, but he produced what amounts to two loops of nine holes, an outer one and an inner one. Little remains of his original design today except that principle. It means that you do not find yourself playing half the course with the wind behind you and then have to force your way back through it. As you play Muirfield, the wind is never from the same direction for long.

Despite its shortcomings, Muirfield was firmly on the Open Championship rota — perhaps, in

the beginning, mostly because it is a mere 15 miles (24 km) or so from Edinburgh. Harold Hilton won in 1892, the second amateur to do so after John Ball, two years before; Bobby Jones is the only other amateur to have won the championship (1930). Four years later saw the arrival of Harry Vardon as a champion, the course by this time considerably lengthened and three or four strokes harder. In 1901, James Braid won his first Open here, and as a memento named a son after the course – Harry Muirfield Braid.

There was a gap in Muirfield Open Championships after 1912, perhaps because the R & A felt the course was a little substandard. However, during the 1920s Muirfield was substantially redesigned to take its present form; the only changes since have concerned bunkering and a very few new tees.

In 1929, Walter Hagen won the last of his four Open titles at Muirfield, and in 1935 the little favoured Alf Perry triumphed. Next, in 1948, came the last of Henry Cotton's three championships, followed by the first of Gary Player's, in 1959. Player thought he had thrown it all away with a double-bogey 6 on the last hole, but he was in luck that day.

The Muirfield Open of 1966 has gone into legend. The rough was so high that Doug Sanders remarked that he would rather have the hay concession than the prize money! General comment was that the course had been set up to reduce the dominance of the power players. Even so, it was the most powerful of them all at that time, Jack Nicklaus, who came through to win his first Open Championship, leaving his driver in the bag most of the time.

In 1972 there came one of the most remarkable British Opens of modern times. Nicklaus, far behind, threw his normal caution to the winds and stormed in with a 65, a round which with a little good fortune might have been even better. Even so, with a couple of holes to play, it seemed that Tony Jacklin would be the winner. With Lee Trevino onto the rear fringe of the 17th in four strokes, Jacklin took four to hole out from only a little pitch short of the flag while Trevino holed his chip shot – one of several outrageous strokes he played during the event. Jacklin then bogeyed the last as well. Trevino won, with Nicklaus finishing second.

Eight years later, in 1980, there was a new world number one, Tom Watson, who gave perhaps the most dominant of his major-

ABOVE The clubhouse, the 18th green and the famous bunker with its island of turf. In the 1987 Open, Paul Azinger took 5 and Nick Faldo a par 4 at this hole. The championship title rested on this one stroke.

LEFT William Inglis, captain of the club between 1782 and 1784.

championship-winning performances. With a third round 64 he spreadeagled the field, and in his final round he gave nothing at all back, winning the event by 4 strokes — and, some thought, humiliating Muirfield in the process with his total of 271.

In the most recent Open Championship, 1987, the weather came to the aid of the course. Though Rodger Davis shot a 64 in the first round to lead by 3, neither Davis nor anyone else repeated that kind of scoring as the winds rose and the rains lashed down. Only seven finished under par for the championship this time, and the champion, Nick Faldo, was the only man not to be above par in any single round.

Although the US entry for the Open Championship has been at a high level since the mid-1960s, often a few of the year's best players do not come. They do, however, inevitably turn out at St Andrews, because of its aura of history, and at Muirfield. In the latter case, they have heard that it is by no means just some joke links course with a lot of bunkers in the 'wrong' places, and sometimes impossible stances when you have rasped a drive down the middle. This is perhaps the reason why Muirfield is now rated so highly: there is very little to dislike. From the tee the troubles ahead are usually plain to the eye. The fairways are not wildly undulating, and neither are the greens. The rough, though it may well look severe, is only really dense after wet, warm weather. Furthermore, to US eyes, it matches modern concepts of golf-course design by having scarcely a blind shot.

Only the depth of the bunkers is controversial. Some think that it should be possible to play a wooden club from a fairway bunker, if a golfer can strike with enough precision. At Muirfield, a sand iron sideways can be the only sensible choice. This, some say, reduces those capable of playing daring long shots from sand to the level of those content to wedge the ball out. The same argument can be put forward regarding the greenside bunkers. These are deep. At Muirfield, although the greens are usually holding enough, you do not see players walking into the sand and looking as if it is going to be a

RIGHT Old Tom Morris designed the original Muirfield layout at the beginning of the 1890s. It has been much changed since.

FAR RIGHT In 1896 Harry Vardon, kneeling, lines up a putt while J H Taylor waits during the play-off for the Open Championship. Two caddies and a marker stand by — but not one spectator!

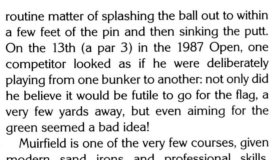

routine matter of splashing the ball out to within a few feet of the pin and then sinking the putt. On the 13th (a par 3) in the 1987 Open, one competitor looked as if he were deliberately playing from one bunker to another: not only did he believe it would be futile to go for the flag, a very few yards away, but even aiming for the green seemed a bad idea!

Muirfield is one of the very few courses, given modern sand irons and professional skills, where players in an Open Championship wonder not how close they can get to the hole but simply if they can get their ball back into play. In 1987, Bernhard Langer, a 3-1 bookmakers' chance after 36 holes, put his second shot into a cross bunker some 30 yards (27 m) short of the green on the 8th; by the time he reached the green he had played 5. His hopes were gone. The day before, Arnold Palmer had seemed to be making the 36-hole cut until he bunkered his second to the 14th and took an interminable 5 to get out.

Difficult holes are not necessarily great ones. Par is hard to get on the 1st, for example, at least partly because targets are not well defined and the hole is more than 440 yards (400 m) long. The par 3s, however, none of them long, are uniformly excellent, and the last six holes supply a test fit for a championship. Good straight shots are needed for the par-3 13th and 16th; the 14th is out of range in two when the wind is against; the 17th is reachable in two as a par 5 only with wind assistance. The 18th, about 450 yards (410 m) from the championship tees, is a hole that sets two challenges: keep out of the fairway bunkers or you will not find the green with your second shot; hit the green with your second or your recovery is not likely to be close to the flag.

MUIRFIELD VILLAGE

MUIRFIELD VILLAGE
COUNTRY CLUB
DUBLIN, OHIO
UNITED STATES

BELOW The 9th green and fairway showing the stream so often in play on this splendid hole.

Jack Nicklaus was very impressed with Scotland's Muirfield when he first played it during the 1959 Walker Cup. He liked its fairness and the fastidious revetment of the bunkers. He was hardly likely to alter his opinions when in 1966 he won the British Open on the same course! For these reasons he decided to name his home-town course for Muirfield. However, the design inspiration in fact came much more from the rolling terrain of Augusta National. Nicklaus wanted to produce an equivalent to Augusta, and this he did in woodlands a few miles outside Columbus.

Although Nicklaus's course was not ready for play until 1974, he was prepared for the next stage of his master plan. This was the Memorial Tournament, which began in 1976. There can be little doubt that Nicklaus aimed for his event

to become a fifth major. This has yet to come about but, backed as it is by his immense prestige, the Memorial, which celebrates the achievements of great players of the past, is currently the most likely event to achieve the status of a major championship.

Constructed with no regard to expense, Muirfield Village has specially prepared vantage points for spectators. As at Augusta, water hazards are a great feature, as are the rewards for bold shot-making on the par 5s. Greens are small and tightly bunkered – one reason why it was not until 1983 that any player managed to break par in every round of the Memorial. Indeed, there had been protests early on from Tour players about the course's difficulty, and Nicklaus had shown himself willing to respond. He swapped the lake in front of the 530-yard

(485-m) 11th for a stream and modified the bunkering to reduce the number of downhill bunker shots with water beyond.

Although such a formidable tournament test, Muirfield Village is designed so that it can be much shortened for everyday play, using different teeing grounds; these are actually separate tees rather than the more common single, long tee. Whatever the length of individual holes, however, the course calls for the use of every club in the bag.

In September 1987 Muirfield Village hosted the Ryder Cup, which was won by Europe. Having built up a commanding lead in the foursomes and fourballs during the first two days, Europe's eventual margin of victory was narrow as the United States fought back superbly in the singles on the last day.

ABOVE The course that Jack built, with Nicklaus himself in play.

RIGHT The treacherously shallow 12th green. This par 3 has some of the features of both the 12th and the 16th at Augusta.

THE NATIONAL

THE NATIONAL GOLF
LINKS OF AMERICA
SOUTHAMPTON
LONG ISLAND
NEW YORK
UNITED STATES

Charles Blair Macdonald was certainly fully convinced of his own importance as a great golf architect. It is no surprise, then, that the name he selected for his masterwork is about as imposing as it could be. However, he had an excuse for his grandiosity. Macdonald from the very start set about designing this course with the highest ambitions – to produce the United States's first great golf course – and he achieved exactly what he set out to do. In some ways it proved superior to any other course in the world at the time.

His preparations were perhaps the most thorough ever. Beginning in 1902, Macdonald paid annual visits across the Atlantic to study UK golf courses. Many have said that he copied what he found and merely reproduced the results at The National, but this was neither his aim nor indeed the truth. Macdonald noted important features of good golf holes and later used what he had learned. At no stage did he ever intend to 'borrow' the 18 best holes in the British Isles and replicate them on Long Island; he did want to have 18 good holes, and he felt that courses like North Berwick West and St Andrews Old were by no means without weak or dull holes. He was, therefore, as eager to find out why bad holes were bad as to analyze why good ones were good.

The names Macdonald gave to his holes at The National show clearly the occasions on which he felt he had imitated a British hole. The 2nd, for example, he called 'Sahara': it was based on the 3rd at Royal St George's. The 3rd, called the 'Alps', was 'borrowed' from the 17th at Prestwick; it too has a blind second shot and a bunker right across the front of the green. The 4th, 'Redan', shares with North Berwick, another Scottish course, the feature of a long green set at an angle to the line of shot and similar bunkering. Two more – the 7th and 13th – borrow Old Course features. The 7th, which he actually called 'St Andrews', uses features of the Road Hole which include a bold carry over bunkers (instead of the old railway sheds), a pot bunker towards the front left of the green, and severe bunkering on the right of the green (substituting for the road at St Andrews). The 13th owes some debt to the 11th at St Andrews, the Eden hole, with some similarity in the front bunkering

and the nearness of water.

Macdonald also took a long time over another part of his painstaking research – finding the right piece of land. He settled for 250 acres (100 ha) or so by the Sebonac and Peconic bays and close by Shinnecock Hills. Work began in 1907, and the course was opened a couple of years later. Originally it was short (by modern standards), at around 6,100 yards (5,580 m). By the mid-1920s, however, it was over 6,500 yards (5,945 m), and today it is over 6,700 yards (6,125 m) – perhaps not quite long enough for PGA Tour events or the US Open. The most important event so far to be held at The National, in fact, has been the 1922 Walker Cup. It was highly praised by both teams then – as, indeed, it had been from the beginning.

Although much has been made of Macdonald's 'borrowings' from overseas, he introduced original features of his own. His little 6th hole, only 130 yards (119 m), may have been the first hole ever to have a green wholly ringed by bunkers, and he also made use of water

carries from the tee (although not close to the greens) at several holes. The classic hole on The National is the 14th, about 360 yards (330 m) in length. The tee shot is played over an arm of the bay to a fairway which doglegs sharply, following the line of the water to a tightly bunkered green which is set quite close to both a road and water. The water carry, however, is not severe, for Macdonald recognized that few club players can hit the ball a distance approaching 200 yards (185 m). Normally in the courses he designed he liked to give short hitters an alternative route; here he simply allowed for their limitations.

Probably Macdonald would have liked, really, to design a links course, but was unable to find suitable land. If he was frustrated in this, he certainly made up for it by the sheer quantity of bunkers he incorporated — there are said to be about 500 of them.

Similarly, since he could not have all his holes close to the sea, he compromised by producing a grand finale, with the last seven holes close to water.

ABOVE LEFT The plain, even severe, clubhouse at the National perhaps reflects Charles Blair Macdonald's love of Scottish simplicity. (© LEONARD KAMSLER ,1985)

ABOVE A view over the course from the clubhouse. (© LEONARD KAMSLER 1985)

LEFT The course was used for the 1922 Walker Cup. Here is Macdonald with Chick Evans (left) and Jess Sweetser (right).

OAK HILL EAST

Before the 1956 US Open, the first that Oak Hill hosted, Ben Hogan had said that the course was not difficult enough for the championship. Perhaps he was right. Cary Middlecoff's 281, the winning total, was the lowest ever up to that time except for Hogan's 276 at Riviera several years before, in 1948. Even so, the cream came to the top, for Middlecoff was followed home by Hogan himself, Julius Boros, Ed Furgol, Peter Thomson and Ted Kroll. In 1968 the championship returned and the scoring was even better, Lee Trevino equalling the record set the year before by Jack Nicklaus at Baltusrol with 275 and scoring every round below 70. After this, the USGA decided that there would have to be changes if the Open was to come again to Oak Hill.

The course was originally designed by Donald Ross in 1926, and it features his much-loved raised greens; also he had thousands of trees planted. After Trevino's win, however, the members agreed with the USGA that there would have to be some alterations, and George and Tom Fazio were called in. They certainly produced one great hole, the 5th, a par 4 of 419 yards (383 m) with a creek all down the right. The creek comes closer as it nears the green before swinging around the green's front and winding down the left side.

The next major championship to come to Oak Hill East was the 1980 US PGA. The course had by now also been 'tricked up' through encouraging rough to grow at the approaches to greens in order to catch a straight shot pitching short. Nicklaus had one of his greatest victories. With the US Open already under his belt that year, when many thought his great days over, he had a 66 in the third round to lead by 3, and then went on to a 7-stroke victory. It was his fifth PGA title and his 19th major championship. Nicklaus was 6 under par but the people at Oak Hill were probably satisfied with the new difficulty of their course: the next best score was Andy Bean's one over.

For the members, Oak Hill is now a very difficult test. If you can cope with the length Oak Hill plays, most other courses will seem shorter. There is very little roll on the fairways, and the rough is very dense. The greens are very fast, but they will always hold a well struck shot.

The start is intimidating, with a couple of long par 4s followed by a 200-yard (183-m) par 3; this means that, for good players, a long iron at least will be needed for all the shots to the greens. Next comes a par 5 of 570 yards (521 m) that even professionals do not expect to reach in two. (There is another par 5 later, the 596-yard [545-m] 13th, that no one has ever reached in two.) In all, there are 10 par 4s that are over 400 yards (365 m), three of them in a row constituting one of the toughest finishes in championship golf. Each of these final three is around the 450-yard (410-m) mark.

ABOVE AND ABOVE RIGHT
Two views of Oak Hill taken before the 1980 PGA Championship which was won so convincingly by Jack Nicklaus. Note the dense texture of the semi-rough, one of the most difficult features of the course. (© TONY ROBERTS 1979)

RIGHT Cary Middlecoff, shown here in practice, won the 1956 US Open at Oak Hill ahead of Ben Hogan and Julius Boros.

OAKLAND HILLS

Tournament players expect to be able to get up in two at par-5 holes. Their great length helps make a steady round seem spectacular. They also used to expect to look out from the tee and feel able to ignore the fairway bunkers – those only trapped club members who strayed to one side or the other. Professionals could fly most of them with ease, which made long driving much less hazardous.

All this changed before the 1951 US Open. Robert Trent Jones was called in to revise Donald Ross's 1917 design of the Oakland Hills course. He threw at the Open competitors bunkers galore, the majority being sited so as to narrow the fairways and positioned so that most competitors could not carry them from the tee. Obsolete fairway bunkers were filled in. The players did not like it and the course was nick-named 'The Monster' after Ben Hogan, having won his third US Open, commented that he was glad he had 'brought this monster to its knees'.

Although Hogan was a very controlled driver by this time in his career, the task had not been easy. His chances seemed to have vanished early on when he bogeyed five of his first nine holes, finishing the round in 76. But he improved on that in every succeeding round – 73, 71, 67. When golfers start chatting about the greatest round of golf ever, that Hogan 67 al-

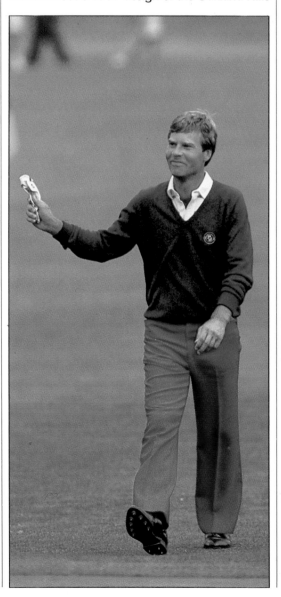

ABOVE Ralph Guldahl at the peak of his career. He won the 1937 US Open over the course, one that Sam Snead, then at the outset of his career, had seemed bound to win.

LEFT The 18th with the clubhouse behind during the climax of the 1985 US Open. (© TONY ROBERTS 1985)

FAR LEFT Ben Crenshaw acknowledges applause for his hole in one during the 1985 US Open at Oakland Hills, but Andy North was the surprise champion.

ways has to come into the reckoning. He played the first nine that day in par, and then came home in 32. The climax came at the 18th, a dogleg of about 460 yards (420 m). Hogan carried the bunkers Jones had set into the angle, fired a mid-iron to about a yard, and won by 2 strokes. In the whole championship only one other competitor broke 70, the late Clayton Heafner: he had a 69 and finished second.

Afterwards, Jones was defensive about his changes. He considered he had achieved what he had set out to do: provide a severe test of professional golf. Perhaps he did indeed start the trend followed ever since by the USGA, that of 'taking the driver out of the game'.

In fact, by the time Jones came along, Oakland Hills had already hosted two Opens. In 1924, the little known English-born Cyril Walker won by 3 strokes from Bobby Jones. But 1937 was a far more significant year in US Open history. Sam Snead seemed to have won – it was the first time he had played in the championship – but Ralph Guldahl came through on the post to win. Snead, despite his plethora of other titles, was never to be US Open champion. How improbable that would have seemed back in 1937!

Since Hogan's year, 1951, there have been two further US Opens at Oakland Hills. The first of these was won by Gene Littler, his only major championship as a professional. The next came in 1985, Andy North winning his second US Open. This too was an oddity: North has won only three tournaments in his career, but two of them have been the US Open.

As Jones intended, the finish from the 14th to the 18th is what most tests players of all levels. Each of the holes (four par 4s and a 200-yard [183-m] par 3) usually demands a long shot to the green. However, Gary Player broke this 'rule' when playing the 400-yard (366-m) 16th in the final round of the 1972 US PGA. He was far to the right in the rough with his tee shot, but on a line which shortened the dogleg. He took out a 9-iron and gave the ball a smash which sent it soaring over the trees and the lake beyond. It came to rest a little more than a yard from the hole.

The 18th, played so well by Ben Hogan in 1951, is a daunting finishing hole. It doglegs gently right, with bunkers in the landing area for the tee shot. The green itself is heavily bunkered, both short and close-up, with a very narrow entrance, and throws off many shots that are good but just not quite good enough.

OAKMONT

OAKMONT COUNTRY
CLUB, OAKMONT
PENNSYLVANIA
UNITED STATES

RIGHT Oakmont
photographed during the
1973 US Open which
was won by Johnny
Miller. (© TONY ROBERTS
1973)

BELOW RIGHT The famous
Church Pews bunkers.

FAR RIGHT William C
Fownes Junior, the son
of Oakmont's founder,
repeatedly redesigned
the course, adding
features to make it
harder and harder to
play. Though still a
challenging course,
Oakmont is less difficult
now than when Fownes
was the supremo.

This course is the product of the labours of
Henry C Fownes, followed by a lifetime's work
from his son William, a US Amateur Champion.
Both were consumed with the idea that a golf
course should be punishing. As the land chosen
by the village of Oakmont, 10 miles (16 km) or
so outside Pittsburgh, had none of the natural
threats of a Pine Valley or Pebble Beach, the
father-and-son architects had to do it through
bunkering and the speed of the greens. Oakmont's bunkers are indeed legendary. Today
there are still nearly 200, and there used to be
more than 300.

But the Fowneses were not satisfied with sand
alone as a hazard. They did not like the idea of
players finding a fairway bunker and then being
able to fire their next onto the green from long
range. Just after World War I, a special rake was
introduced at Oakmont. The idea was not to
leave the sand unblemished but rather to make
lies more difficult. After the green-staff had departed satisfied, the sand was deliberately well
furrowed: almost all shots rolled into the troughs
so that the hapless golfer had very near the
same thing as a buried lie.

Some professionals complained. They made
the valid point that such practices took the skill
out of recovery shots: all anyone could do was
blast out. After World War II, however, the furrows became less severe and today they are a
thing of the past. The river sand too has departed – players found that more difficult as well.
It has now been replaced by the brilliant white
sand demanded by most US golfers.

It is no wonder that there were such a vast
number of bunkers on the course. If William
Fownes noticed that players could carry one
from the tee or, nearer to the green, were escap-
ing their just deserts after inferior shots, he
would simply order another bunker to be constructed!

There have been fewer changes to the greens:
these were designed to be terrifyingly fast, and
they remain so. In the early days, barrels of sand
were used as well as a 1500 lb (680 kg) roller, a
practice probably unprecedented. In one way or
another problems of soil compaction were
avoided, or at least overcome, and Oakmont
had greens receptive only to very well struck

shots. The greens were also, aided by cutters set to about $3/32$ inch (2·4 mm), terrifyingly fast to putt. A player once claimed that he had marked his ball with a dime, but that the coin had slid off the green . . .

Bobby Jones was surely the likely man to cope with fast greens, yet in Oakmont's first US Open, played in 1927 just after the first Ryder Cup match, the course beat him. His best round was a 76 and, for once, he finished down the field. (Tommy Armour won after a play-off with a total of 301.) The next Open at Oakmont came in 1935. The winner, Sam Parks, was the only man to break 300 – he did it by just 1. The runner-up, long-hitting Jimmy Thomson, was destroyed by the 17th. He drove to the green, then a distance of about 290 yards (265 m), and when his putt was a foot (30 cm) or so from the hole he thought it would drop for an eagle 2. Alas, in the end he needed four putts.

Oakmont was tamed but not defeated in the next two US Opens held there. In 1953, Ben Hogan was at his all-time peak. He began with a 67 but Sam Snead, 5 behind at that point, began to overhaul him. Hogan's last four holes of par, par, birdie and birdie were too good for Snead, who finished 6 strokes behind. Hogan's astonishing 283 was equalled by Jack Nicklaus and Arnold Palmer in 1962. Nicklaus had been a professional only a few months and was without a victory. He tied with Palmer, who had the support of most of the crowd, and then won the 18-hole play-off by 3 strokes.

Oakmont's first 'defeat' came in 1973. In his final round, Johnny Miller came from 6 back, and his 63 set a new record. However, we have to add the qualification that rains had made the greens soft and receptive and taken the fear out of putting.

Oakmont's most recent Open, in 1983, also featured a great move from behind, this time by Larry Nelson. At halfway, his 148 left him close to missing the cut, but he responded with 65 and 67 to beat Tom Watson by 1 stroke.

Although some of Oakmont's sharpest teeth have been drawn, it remains one of the great tests of shot-making, and has two dramatic hazards. Between the 3rd and 4th fairways lies the Church Pews, a very long bunker divided up by eight strips of turf. Leading up to the 8th green is another formidable specimen, 'Sahara': this is over 120 yards (110 m) long and about 30 yards (27 m) wide.

WILLIAM C FOWNES

ROBERT TRENT JONES
born 1906

Although born in England, Jones emigrated to America when about five years old. A good golfer while still a teenager, he was from the start interested in a career as a golf course architect and even designed his own programme of studies at university to equip himself. He did his first work while still at Cornell and rapidly became a full-time architect. Since that time Jones has designed hundreds of courses all over the world. Features of his work include vast teeing areas, testing undulations on greens, extensive use of water hazards and bunkering in dramatic shapes.

For long the world's most famous architect, Jones attracted enormous publicity by his controversial changes to Oakland Hills, Birmingham, Michigan, for the 1951 US Open. Though it wasn't what Ben Hogan had in mind, he probably did Jones a favour by calling the redesign 'a monster'.

Throughout his long career Jones has shown that it is possible to create high-class golf courses on any kind of land; draining swamps, blasting through rock and cutting through jungle. He has designed, or contributed to, several of the courses in this book. The greatest work of his old age will probably prove to be the new course at Ballybunion in County Kerry, Ireland.

CECIL HUTCHISON

ROBERT TRENT JONES

BOBBY JONES
1902 - 71

Though Jones was the greatest golfer of his day, he never became highly involved in golf course design, perhaps because he would have been working during the Depression years when courses were being closed down rather than built. Nevertheless, he was involved in the development of Augusta from its beginnings to the time of his death. With Alister Mackenzie, he seems to have cooperated mainly in giving his thoughts on how the course would test the best players and also be enjoyable for the less talented.

Much later, he was involved in the design of the par-3 course at Augusta and Peachtree, with Robert Trent Jones, also in Georgia.

BOBBY JONES

C B MACDONALD
1856 - 1939

Having learned his golf at St Andrews, Macdonald had no real opportunity to play the game until it was revived in the United States at the end of the 1880s. Macdonald was soon at the forefront of developments as player, administrator and golf architect, the latter a term he coined. His first design was in Chicago which in 1893 had the first 18-hole course in the United States. Moving to New York, he had the ambition to build a great golf course. He studied British courses and noted the features which made for great golf holes and the result was the National Golf Links of America, on Long Island, New York, perhaps the most splendid (or grandiose) name ever given a golf course. Macdonald thought he had created the best golf course in the world and, at the time, perhaps he was right.

As 1895 US Amateur Champion and with the prestige of The National behind him, he was asked to produce other designs. Amongst his most famous were The Lido, which involved major re-shaping of the landscape and Mid-Ocean on Bermuda. Macdonald did not merely imitate the best features of British linksland golf but produced original design ideas of his own, especially the use of water as a hazard and 'island' greens surrounded by sand.

C B MACDONALD

OLYMPIC LAKESIDE

THE OLYMPIC COUNTRY CLUB, SAN FRANCISCO CALIFORNIA UNITED STATES

RIGHT Crowds are massed around the final green during the 1987 US Open. Although Scott Simpson won the title, many thought it was more significant that Tom Watson returned to championship form and went on to win a US tour event later the same year.

Some 20 years ago, three branches were lopped from a tree at Olympic. According to legend, 150 balls fell out.

Olympic is indeed a course of trees, even though it is just 500 yards (460 m) from the Pacific Ocean. From the tees, great and handicap players alike need to consider fairway bunkers just once, on the 6th hole; trees, on the other hand, are a constant menace and make the course one of the tightest and most claustrophobic in the world. The trees do not merely line the fairways but overhang them, ready to block the aerial route.

Once they have escaped the trees they are confronted by the camber of the fairways. The Lakeside course is built on a hillside. Nearly all the holes run side by side across the line of the slope. To hold many of the fairways you need to use a left-to-right shot; hookers are nearly always in trouble unless they can succeed in hitting along exactly the right line. Shots that drift badly off-line finish in the dense trees, the only option often being to try to regain the fairway.

The rough — unlike that at, say, Augusta National — is very severe. During the 1955 US Open Ben Hogan once took three strokes just to move his ball back to the fairway with a wedge, and Arnold Palmer lost the 1966 US Open through attempting to play long irons out instead of a safer club. This severity of the rough is a product of the damp Pacific air, and it means that the Lakeside course plays much longer than its 6,700 yards (6,125 m). The ball does not fly as far, and when it pitches, according to the members, you get a couple of yards of run ... but backwards!

The greens are among the smallest in championship golf, but they are severely bunkered only on the short par 3s — the 8th and the 15th.

The course was first laid out during World War I, reputedly by three immigrant club professionals. A few years later it was bought by the Olympic Country Club, who immediately set about converting the land from a sandy wilderness to what it is today — a course apparently carved out of a forest. Some 20,000 trees were planted, and were later joined by another 10,000. The professional at the time was Sam Whiting, who carried out the design thoughts of Willie Watson, a Scottish immigrant with whom he designed Olympic's other course, the Ocean. As Whiting did not retire until 1954, day-to-day credit should go to him.

The 16th breaks the convention that the fade is the shot that pays off; here a long draw helps to shorten the 604 yards (551 m). Although the green is not punitively guarded by its two flank bunkers, it is said that only Bobby Jones has ever been home in two: he must have been able to drive across the angle of the dogleg over trees that had yet to reach their maturity. In championship play, the 17th is shortened from a relatively undemanding par 5 of 517 yards (473 m) (although that distance is uphill) to the far more daunting prospect of a par 4 of 443 yards (405 m) with a green which is both well bunkered and designed to receive a pitched third rather than a second shot played with a long iron.

The best hole, however, is probably the 18th, a par 4 of just 330 yards (300 m) or so. The trouble appears to be on the left for the tee shot, but the fairway runs away to the right, from where overhanging trees will block out many pitched second shots.

Olympic has hosted three US Opens. The first two brought shock results. In 1955, Ben Hogan seemed to have won a record fifth US Open when the totally unknown Jack Fleck — from a municipal course at Davenport, Iowa — managed to birdie the last hole to tie Hogan's total. Even so, no one gave Fleck a chance in the 18-hole play-off, but he held a 1-stroke lead on the final tee where Hogan, who had learned to fade the ball almost infallibly, then hooked into the deepest rough on the course and took three more to regain the fairway, saying goodbye to his championship hopes en route. Eleven years later, in 1966, Arnold Palmer seemed set to break the US Open record four-round aggregate with nine holes to play. Would Jack Nicklaus or Billy Casper be second? But Palmer, who had been hitting straight or with a little fade all week, then hooked a few and lost a 7-stroke lead. Casper and Palmer tied and, in the 18-hole play-off, Palmer again lost an early lead, Casper in the end winning by 4 strokes.

In 1987, Olympic became the first Californian course to have hosted the US Open three times. Although the early lead was taken by Ben Crenshaw, the Championship was a battle between Seve Ballesteros, Tom Watson and the eventual winner, Scott Simpson.

JAMES BRAID

GEORGE CRUMP

WILLIE FERNIE

HERBERT FOWLER

JAMES BRAID
1870 - 1950

Though the Great Triumvirate of Braid, Vardon and Taylor should have been in great demand as golf architects, Vardon produced few courses and most of Taylor's were really the work of his partner, Fred Hawtree. It was a very different matter with Braid, Open Champion five times in the first decade of the century. After World War I, he became the most prolific designer in Britain, being equally active in both England and Scotland at a time when most architecture was being carried out by good amateur golfers rather than professionals.

Although Braid is most known today for the Gleneagles courses, where he was greatly helped by the very favourable terrain and superb surroundings, he was just as able to work with less promising ground.

GEORGE CRUMP
died 1918

Crump has but one golf course to his credit, one which was unfinished at his death. His vision was to find a stretch of land which would yield a great golf course. He did and today we have Pine Valley, New Jersey.

WILLIE FERNIE
1851 - 1924

Open Champion in 1883, having tied and lost the play-off the previous year. Fernie was professional at Troon, Scotland, for well over 30 years from 1887. He developed that championship course and, amongst a few other designs, created the original course at Turnberry, Ayrshire, Scotland.

HERBERT FOWLER
1856 - 1941

Although not taking to golf until early middle age, Fowler rapidly became good enough to reach the later stages of the British Amateur Championship. His chance in golf architecture came when he was asked to design Walton Heath, near London, early this century. This rapidly became a famous course with a highly impressive membership list. David Lloyd George and Winston Churchill were amongst those who played there; Churchill rather reluctantly as he preferred conversation. Much work came Fowler's way as a result of this golfing and social success, and Westward Ho! was one of the courses he made considerable changes to. Fowler also worked in the United States, mainly in California. Apart from Walton Heath, his most respected courses are probably Cruden Bay in Scotland and The Berkshire to the west of London.

WILLIAM C FOWNES
1878 - 1950

A good enough golfer to win the US Amateur Championship and play for the first Walker Cup team, Fownes was a one-course man and constantly concerned himself with improving Oakmont, in Pennsylvania. This meant, in one instance, creating new bunkering when he found players able to drive them from the tee and bringing a rake into use to create furrows which made long recovery shots virtually impossible from his bunkers. He was also a believer in extremely fast greens and certainly succeeded in producing them at Oakmont. He was president of the USGA during the 1920s.

CECIL HUTCHISON
1877 - 1941

Hutchison was a top amateur golfer in the years from the turn of the century up to World War I. His greatest achievement was to be runner-up in the 1909 British Amateur Championship, losing one down at Muirfield to a fellow member of the Honourable Company of Edinburgh Golfers.

Eventually turning to golf course design after army service, Hutchison worked on the course at Prince's, Kent. However, he is best known today for his work at Turnberry, Ayrshire, Scotland.

DR LAIDLAW PURVES
1843 - 1918

A good club-level golfer, Laidlaw Purves had learned his golf in Scotland and later, while a surgeon at Guy's Hospital in London, was an influential member at Wimbledon. Dissatisfied with the golfing terrain there, he set out to survey the south coast of England to find more suitable land. In due course he climbed the tower of St Clement's church in Sandwich, Kent, and saw the promised land – a fine stretch of duneland which was to become three golf courses, Royal Cinque Ports at Deal, Royal St George's and Prince's.

There is little doubt that he played the major role in the original layout of St George's. However, though he designed a ladies' course on Wimbledon Common and also Littlestone, he made little provision for them at St George's and to this day the club remains one of the most restrictive in Britain. It was not until the 1920s that any facilities were provided. Later the famous notice was posted: 'Ladies are authorized to wear trousers for golf provided that they take them off before entering the Clubhouse'.

DR LAIDLAW PURVES

DONALD ROSS
1872 - 1948

The most prolific architect of good golf courses ever, Ross was born at Dornoch in Sutherland, Scotland, and later used much of what he had learned of 'natural' course design in his work in the United States.
Ross served an apprenticeship in clubmaking at St Andrews before emigrating to the United States toward the end of the century to work at a Boston club, from where he began to work in the winter at Pinehurst, N Carolina. His course work at this winter resort attracted many visitors and led to ever-increasing design commissions. Ross is credited with several hundred US courses.

STANLEY THOMPSON
1894 - 1952

Scottish by birth, Thompson became active in Canadian golf course architecture shortly after World War I and famous for his designs for two Canadian Railway companies. The courses were Banff Springs, Alberta, and Jasper Park, Ontario, both set in a mountain context.
The designer of many courses in Canada, Thompson also worked in the USA and South America.

DONALD ROSS

STANLEY THOMPSON

A W TILLINGHAST

A W TILLINGHAST
1874 - 1942

A good amateur golfer, 'Tillie', as he was often known, may well have picked up many of his architectural ideas while in Scotland as a young man.
The majority of his work was done during the golf boom years of the 1920s when opportunities were at a peak. By contrast, relatively few courses were built by anybody during the Depression years.
A W Tillinghast was perhaps the greatest US architect of his day and his fame revived in modern times when it was realised how many courses of championship standard he had built. Some well-known names are Baltusrol, Inverness, Quaker Ridge and Winged Foot.

HUGH WILSON
1879 - 1925

Wilson's reputation rests on one course, the East at Merion, Ardmore, Pennsylvania. Yet this may well be considered the greatest course ever created without massive earth-moving on none too suitable ground. He also designed Merion's West course and did a little other architectural work, including the completion of Crump's course at Pine Valley, New Jersey.

HUGH WILSON

REAT

CHITECTS •

DR ALISTAIR MACKENZIE
1870 - 1934

Although qualified as a doctor, Mackenzie eventually gave up medicine in his late 30s to concentrate on golf course design.

Before World War I he was mainly active in England and during the war, serving in the Royal Engineers, showed brilliant use of camouflage designs. This skill was put to use in his golf course designs, where he sometimes cunningly concealed the difficulties of holes.

After the war Mackenzie increasingly worked outside Great Britain especially in Australia and the United States. Three of his courses are featured in this book – Royal Melbourne, Cypress Point and Augusta National. You would find plenty of supporters to argue that each of these is the greatest in the world. Certainly a few of the holes at Cypress Point are amongst the most photographed and, through annual exposure of the Masters on television, the last nine holes at Augusta must be the most well known stretch of golf course in the world. Mackenzie believed that a good course must be suitable for players of every level and in this sense Augusta is possibly his greatest triumph. It tests championship level golfers to the limit while the more ordinary players quite often find they score better than at their home club.

DR ALISTAIR MACKENZIE

TOM MORRIS
1821 - 1908

Invariably referred to as 'Old Tom' to distinguish him from his more brilliant son (as a professional golfer), Morris was the first man to be in great demand as a golf course designer. Many great links course, including Westward Ho!, Muirfield and Royal County Down are today credited to him though they have been drastically changed since he first laid them out. Even so, many of the green sites he chose remain in use to this day.

JACK NEVILLE

TOM MORRIS

JACK NEVILLE
1895 - 1978

Neville designed a few courses which were never built and later in life at least two that were. He was never a practising golf course architect, however, it was almost pure chance that he created one of the world's greatest courses at Pebble Beach. Neville was employed selling real estate for a company developing land on the Monterey Peninsula, California when he was asked to design a golf course. The result was Pebble Beach. He is said to have spent three weeks walking the land, working out the route of the course during the 1920s. Though there have been changes of detail since, Pebble Beach remains substantially as Neville made it. He said that the course was always there – he simply found the holes.

Neville was a very good amateur golfer.

JACK NICKLAUS

JACK NICKLAUS
born 1940

To be a great golfer means, in golf architecture, very little. Such a man should certainly have a grasp of what shots are the most demanding for the superior player but may fail to grasp the principles of making courses enjoyable for far humbler golfers. Nicklaus has succeeded in creating courses which are successful on both counts.

One of the very few men to set out on a professional golfing career with the aim of being the greatest player ever, Nicklaus may well also wish to be an immortal architect. With Bobby Jones as his rival as a golfer, the only one, Nicklaus's Muirfield Village could become a rival to Augusta as *the* great inland course and seems to have been inspired by his desire to create a great course in his home state, Ohio.

In Great Britain, his course near Plymouth, Devon, has created enormous interest but his main practice is in the United States, where Shoal Creek, Birmingham, Alabama, has been used for a PGA Championship. Nicklaus has earlier worked with both Desmond Muirhead and Pete Dye, both prominent figures in golf architecture today.

PEBBLE BEACH

PEBBLE BEACH

MONTEREY PENINSULA

CALIFORNIA

UNITED STATES

RIGHT The 6th and 7th holes at Pebble Beach are precariously positioned on a peninsula jutting into the Pacific.

Among the accepted great courses of the world, Pebble Beach has to be the unanimous choice as the most spectacular. Like the classic early Scottish links courses, it is an out-and-back layout with the 11th at the far end of the course. The first three holes are inland, but the 4th and then the 6th to the 10th run along the cliffs of Carmel Bay. The 11th heads inland again and the 13th to the 16th move back toward the clubhouse. They are set among pines, eucalyptus, oaks and cypresses. Although all the inland holes are good, they lack the drama of the ones on the clifftops. The 17th returns to the shore and the 18th curves along beside the Pacific.

A real-estate salesman called Jack Neville was an amateur good enough to win the California Championship five times and to be picked for the Walker Cup team in 1923. People have always been apt to think that good golfers design good courses. This is far from always true, but property developer Sam Morse made no mistake when in 1918 he asked Neville to create a golf course for him. Neville later said: 'The golf course was there all the time. All I did was find the holes.' He spent weeks walking the land until he had decided the route and the sites for the greens. He then called in another amateur, Douglas Grant, for consultations on the subject of bunkering.

Neville certainly started with a superb piece of golfing territory. Nevertheless, it is to his credit that he produced a masterpiece. No one since has suggested anything by way of drastic alteration.

For very good golfers, Pebble Beach is a course demanding heroic shots; for the less good, however, there are usually safer routes to play the holes if you accept the loss of a stroke to par. Those heroic shots all come on the Pacific holes. The 4th is a comparatively gentle introduction, a short par 4 of just 325 yards (297 m), but even so it has the cliffs close by for any approach shot that leaks to the right. The 6th, like nearly all par 5s, is not particularly difficult, and there is the reward, as you approach the green, of one of the great golf-course views – away along the cliff-line to the 10th green. From here on, though, heroics are called for.

The 7th is only 120 yards (110 m) long and

ABOVE The majestic sweep of the par-5 18th is here viewed from behind the green. From the tee the player has to decide how far he dare play out across the ocean. Even so, this hole is not a frightener, unless there is a wind towards the sea.

RIGHT Bobby Jones could have been in worse trouble on the 6th during the 1929 US Amateur Championship – he could have been in this sea!

FAR RIGHT The 8th at Pebble Beach is one of the great par 4s of world golf.

downhill, but its green is angled across the line of shot and, like all the others at Pebble Beach, very small. On a calm day, you require 'feel' for the correct length of shot. When the wind is up, judgement too is needed – the Pacific will glee-fully swallow your ball should your shot be played with too strong a club. The 8th is one of the great par 4s of world golf. The tee shot is blind – not usually a recommendation in modern times – and must be weighted short of the chasm ahead . . . but not too short, for that will make the second shot more difficult by far. This shot Jack Nicklaus has called 'the finest second shot on any golf course I have seen'. If you have judged your tee shot to perfection you then have to carry a rocky inlet and some 180 yards (165 m) to the green. The 9th and 10th demand no such carries but are stern in length: both are over 430 yards (395 m), and often they must be played into the wind. The lines which shorten the holes and ease the second shots are close to the cliff edge. Alas, the slopes are in that direction too; few golfers can expect to judge the run of the ground with the requisite precision.

The 17th is much the same medicine as the 7th, but longer – much longer, in fact, at nearly 220 yards (200 m). As before, the waisted green lies across the line of shot, and it is tightly bun-kered. Hitting through the back is not fatal this time, but sending anything far to the left or right

is. The hole cost Arnold Palmer, at the height of his career, a 9 during the 1964 Crosby Tournament.

The 18th is a par 5. Tournament players expect to two-putt most par 5s and score birdies. This is possible here, but for many years it used to be said that no one had ever reached the hole in two. The hole offers a classic tee shot, where golfers have to decide how good they are and how far they can hit the ball as they face either a long or a short carry — the choice is the golfer's own — over an inlet. 'Left and long' is the bold line, but it is possible to go out of bounds playing for safety to the right; even a little too far to the right may well produce the result that a tall pine blocks the second shot. If all has gone well after the tee shot, you must keep your second shot reasonably close to the cliff edge or you will find trees in your way for your approach to the green.

In 1929, Bobby Jones was the greatest golfer in the world and, although an amateur, had recently won the US Open for the third time. In the first round of the 1929 US Amateur at Pebble Beach, however, he was dismissed by the unknown Johnny Goodman. Goodman was himself eliminated from the competition the same day, but a few years later he was to be the last amateur (to date) to win the US Open.

The 8th, 9th and 10th may well be the toughest short sequence of par 4s in the world. Championships are often settled here. Nicklaus, with pars on the first two, held a 4-stroke lead in the final round of the 1972 US Open. When he landed twice on the beach at the 10th, his lead was cut to a single stroke. Was it consolation that a US Ryder Cup player had taken 19 on this hole some years before? After this alarm, a 6 at a par 4, Nicklaus made the championship his with one of the best 1-irons ever played to the 17th. Into a stiff breeze, it was on line all the way, bit, checked, ran into the flag and came to rest about 6 inches (15 cm) from the hole. Even so, his 290 is the second highest winning total in the Open during the past 50 years.

Ten years later, Nicklaus was in pursuit of a record-breaking fifth US Open Championship. Only Watson had a chance of catching him, but then apparently threw it away by sending his tee shot at the 17th into dense greenside rough where he could not hope to stop his little downhill pitch shot close to the hole. Perhaps not. Watson's solution to this little difficulty was to hole it.

PENINA

PENINA GOLF HOTEL

MONTE DE ALVOR

PENINA, PORTIMÃO

ALGARVE, PORTUGAL

ABOVE The late Sir Henry Cotton designed a golf masterpiece at Penina (RIGHT) out of former paddy fields.

Golf course designers have to practise their craft on very unlikely terrain at times. When the late Sir Henry Cotton first visited the proposed site at Penina in 1963, he was confronted by an absolutely flat rice paddy field. Not surprisingly, it was also water-logged. Yet the course he created – the first in the Algarve, opening in 1966 – will probably come to be seen as his monument.

A designer such as Robert Trent Jones might have decided to change the landscape. Cotton, however, took a different approach: he decided to plant thousands of trees, said to total more than 350,000. The purpose in this was two-fold, one reason was that they would help to absorb the excess water and the other was that they were to be the main feature of his new course. They both line the fairways and help create the doglegged holes. However, trees alone could not drain the former paddy fields and another feature that much affects play are the drainage canals. These often border fairways, swing across the front of greens or are close to hand at either side.

Cotton was determined that his course should not be made a nonsense of by the increasing carry of the modern ball. He therefore built vast tees, up to 100 yards (90 m) in length, an idea he probably took from Robert Trent Jones. The result is that although good amateurs can play Penina at under 6,900 yards (6,310 m), it can be stretched to nearly 7,500 yards (6,860 m). One of the longest courses in the world, even the ultimate power hitters are still left with distance to cover for their shots to the greens. These are usually elevated above fairway level and at their best are as good as anywhere in the world.

Cotton lived at the Penina Hotel for many years, leaving temporarily during the Portuguese 'revolution' when he was in disfavour as 'a wealthy Englishman who works too hard'. His last days were saddened when it was announced that the course would be changed by another hand. It now, however, seems that the modifications will not devastate his original design.

When Cotton died just before Christmas in 1987 his knighthood, the first awarded a golfer, had still to be announced in the New Year's Honours list, though he had learned of it some time before. Sir Henry was buried at Penina.

PINEHURST NUMBER TWO

PINEHURST HOTEL AND
COUNTRY CLUB
PINEHURST
NORTH CAROLINA
UNITED STATES

BELOW The clubhouse at the Pinehurst golf complex.

Back in 1895 a Massachusetts businessman, James W. Tufts, was planning to build up a resort where northerners could escape the inclemencies of winter. He settled for the mild, dry climate of North Carolina at Pinehurst, where he bought about 5,000 acres (2,000 ha) of sandhill country at $1 an acre, a bargain if ever there was one.

Golf was not his prime objective, but before the end of the century the explosion in the game's popularity in the United States inspired him to open a nine-hole lay-out, soon expanded to 18 holes. At the end of 1900 he brought the Scotsman Donald Ross, from Dornoch in Sutherland, down from Boston as winter professional. The high quality of the golf at Pinehurst stems from that appointment. Ross went on to become one of the greatest names in golf architecture, but it was at Pinehurst that he gave his most detailed attention to golf, devoting himself almost passionately to what came to be the No. 2 course.

This was opened in 1907 but initially measured only 5,800 yards (5,300 m) or so. It did not approach anything like its present form for nearly 20 years, and it was to continue to have sand greens until the mid-1930s: it was maintained that these were so good that to sow them with Bermuda grass would actually reduce the quality of the putting surfaces. Almost as a footnote, it is worth mentioning that during summer 1987 Jack Nicklaus was hired to replace the greens' Bermuda grass with bent and to substitute a hybrid Bermuda on the fairways.

Donald Ross not only rebuilt the course he found on his arrival and created the No. 2 course, he produced two more 18-hole courses so that, shortly after the end of World War I, Pinehurst became probably the world's first golf complex to have 72 holes.

Perhaps the first great player to come to Pinehurst was Harry Vardon, who played an exhibition match during his countrywide tour in 1900. The following year, the North and South amateur event was begun; it continues to this day. Among its winners have been not one but two Nicklauses. Jack won in 1959 and was a spectator in 1985 when his son, Jack II, took the title.

Two years after the amateur event, in 1903, the professional North and South was started. For a long time it was one of the most prestigious tournaments in US professional golf, but in due course it waned, finally dying in 1951: the basic reason for its demise was that Pinehurst is not close to a major population centre, so that spectators – and hence sponsors – are hard to attract.

In that same year, 1951, however, the Ryder Cup came to Pinehurst. At the time, however, this contest attracted little interest in the United States because the result seemed too easy to predict. Beforehand, Henry Longhurst expressed the general sentiment when he forecast that Great Britain and Ireland would win one of the four foursomes and two of the eight singles. He was not far out: the actual result was United States 9½, Britain and Ireland 2½!

One of the great names playing in that match was Ben Hogan. His play on one hole has become a part of Pinehurst legend. Hogan was playing against Charlie Ward, a short hitter but a player with perhaps the best short game on the British/Irish team. After 25 holes, Ward had managed to hold Hogan to a two-hole lead. They exchanged birdies on the next two holes, but Hogan really settled the match on the 10th hole of the second round. This was listed on the card as 593 yards (542 m), but some thought that this was merely because Pinehurst did not wish to admit that its course included a truly monstrous hole of well over 600 yards (550 m) – perhaps as much as 630 yards (576 m). Even the long hitters were taking a couple of cracking woods and a mid-iron to reach the green. Ward played the hole with two woods and a long iron; Hogan hooked into the trees, wedged out, hit a wood to the front of the green and holed a monster putt for the birdie. This feat probably broke Ward's spirit.

Pinehurst No. 2 was also the scene of Hogan's first win on Tour, at the quite advanced age of 28. On Tuesday 19 March 1940 he began with birdies on three of the first four holes and was round in 66; he was 3 strokes in the lead, his eventual margin of victory after 72 holes. From that time on there was never any stopping him.

The course that Ross created – making a change here and a change there over the years – is not dramatic in the sense of a Pebble Beach or a Turnberry. No single hole, indeed, is blatantly a supreme test. The driving is to quite wide fairways, and the rough is not severe. If you

wander a long way off-line you will inevitably be among the pines which offer seclusion to every hole, and the trees are often set close, so that there are no broad avenues for escape as at, for example, Augusta. There are also clumps of the lovegrass Ross planted, and you have every chance of finding that your ball is resting on an unwelcome bed of pine needles.

However, it is the shots to the greens that provide the main challenges. Most of the greens are raised and contoured, so that a long-iron which is good, but not quite good enough, will gently drift off with the run of the ground into a greenside bunker or among the humps and hollows Ross built as another type of hazard. It is this last feature which makes Pinehurst No. 2 one of the great tests of chipping in the world. If the US Open were ever to come here, there would be no need specially to ring the greens with collars of rough!

ABOVE Spring time at Pinehurst is a visual delight.

PINE VALLEY

PINE VALLEY GOLF CLUB

CLEMENTON

NEW JERSEY

UNITED STATES

The dream of a Philadelphia hotelier, George Crump, Pine Valley is a stranger to tournament golf yet is recognized as one of the very greatest courses in the world, and the most penal of all.

Crump sold his hotel in 1912 and moved out to the site. For a while, he lived in a tent, later in a bungalow. In a couple of years – by 1914 – he had 11 holes roughed out, and by 1916 14 were ready for play. George Crump was one of the great amateur architects; although he did bring H. S. Colt out from the UK for a while to help with the routing of the course, Colt gave his approval to what Crump was doing. A very great deal of work had been needed, especially in the removal of tree-stumps: it is said they stopped counting at 22,000, and there were plenty more after that! With four holes still to be made, however, Crump died early in 1918. His dream course was still a year from completion.

Once play began in 1919, it was not until 1922 that anyone managed to get round in 70. That score was not beaten until just before World War II, when the US Ryder Cup player Ed Dudley had a record 68; later in the same event he had an 85!

However, Pine Valley has been the scene of perhaps the most phenomenal feat of scoring ever. A good-class amateur, J Wood Platt, began with a birdie on the 1st hole and followed this up by eagling the 2nd. He then holed his tee shot on the 3rd and birdied the 4th. Platt was 6 under par after four holes. Alas, he had no return for the round. Perhaps overcome by the enormity of his achievement, Platt retired to the clubhouse to have a quick drink and consider his next move. He never reappeared. Although the tale takes some believing, geography favours it: golfers do indeed pass close to the clubhouse between the 4th green and the 5th tee.

Although Pine Valley is not suited to tournament play because of the lack of room for spectators, it has twice hosted the Walker Cup – in 1936 and 1985. Great Britain and Ireland were trounced by the United States on the first occasion, but the second match was closely fought out, with a win for the United States.

Pine Valley is in sandy pine-forest country. George Crump's approach was to leave the sandy wastes largely alone and to plant island fairways, so that for a great part of the time a golfer has to try to advance from one green patch to the next. If any of these 'hops' fail, the ball tends to be either lost in water or lying unkindly in an unraked wilderness. Perfect play will produce a steady flow of pars, but minor error can be – and often is – savagely punished. Club members used to bet that no visitor would break 80 on a first attempt at the course and that even competent club golfers would fail to break 100.

All great courses seem to include a superb selection of par 3s. Pine Valley's are as good as anywhere. The first of these is the 185-yard (169-m) 3rd – which, if you recall, 'Woody' Platt played in a single stroke! There are two oases of green – the tee and the putting surface – and between the two lies a sandy waste; the green itself is surrounded by more of the same. The 5th is an even sterner test of some 220 yards (200 m) from a high tee over a ravine and water to an elevated green. The 10th, at 145 yards (133 m), should be easier if only on account of its shorter length, but in fact the green is protected all around by very deep bunkers, one at the front being particularly insidious: it 'gathers' shots, and many golfers opt for playing out of it backwards. The 14th is the last of the par 3s and is played over scrub, water and bunkers to an island green; at 185 yards (169 m), it is as demanding as any of the others.

There are only two par 5s at Pine Valley, but one is perhaps the most famous hole on the course. It measures 585 yards (535 m), and has a sandy waste beginning about 280 yards (255 m) out and stretching for about 150 yards (137 m). Even the very longest hitters must aim to play short of this, while short hitters have very little chance of carrying 'Hell's Half Acre' with their second shot. It is thought that the green has never been reached in two – something that is true also of the 600-yard (550-m) 15th.

There are no weak holes among the par 4s. The 13th, at nearly 450 yards (410 m), is perhaps typical of them, with the drive being to an island in the sand. After that, the very long second to the green must carry sand all the way. The 18th is a fitting last hole. Once again, there is a wilderness to carry, and the second shot must carry over a rise liberally set with bunkers.

ABOVE George Crump built one of the world's most punishing courses, but died shortly before its completion.

RIGHT The 5th, a par 3 of over 200 yards (180 m), gives the golfer little margin for error.

PRESTWICK

PRESTWICK GOLF CLUB
PRESTWICK, AYRSHIRE
SCOTLAND

Prestwick is the original home of the Open Championship, although neither course nor club can claim to be one of the original homes of golf in Scotland.

There is a tradition that a monk from Crossraguel and the Lord of Culzean played a legendary challenge match in medieval times, and more regular golf was certainly in progress by the 1830s or 1840s; players paid 10 shillings a year to the Freemen of Prestwick for the privilege. The club was founded in 1851 and a couple of years later Old Tom Morris was invited to come over from his native St Andrews to be the professional. Tom Morris was to become the first really busy golf-course architect and, as one of the leading players of the time, no doubt had influence on the development of the original 12-hole lay-out. By the time Old Tom returned to St Andrews, Prestwick had become the best course in the country and his son Tommy, to go down in history as Young Tom Morris, had learned to play the game here.

The Open Championship had also begun. It was organized by Prestwick Golf Club and first played on 17 October 1860 with just eight competitors. Willie Park Sr won, Old Tom coming second. All the early championships were played at Prestwick until Young Tom caused a change. He won three years in a row during 1868–70; under the rules the trophy, a splendid belt, became his permanently. A one-year pause ensued, partly because money was being collected for the present trophy, a silver claret jug. When the championship resumed, the R & A and the Honourable Company of Edinburgh Golfers, who then played at Musselburgh, had joined the enterprise, increasing the number of courses available.

Championships continued to be played periodically at Prestwick, however, until 1925, by which time 24 Opens had been settled over the course. In that year, a Scottish-American, Macdonald Smith, went into the final round with a 5-stroke lead but collapsed with an 82, his concentration destroyed, it is said, by the wildly surging crowds.

This last Prestwick Open made it clear that the course could not accommodate large crowds packed into a small space, particularly on the last four holes. The Open will almost certainly never return.

Yet there are compensations. The course was expanded to 18 holes in 1883, but there have been relatively few changes since. Even more than at St Andrews, visitors feel they are playing traditional golf. Blind shots, for instance, are generally frowned on today, yet you will find plenty of them still at Prestwick — some of them having to be struck over high sand dunes. Another feature is that the greens are often hidden away in hollows, perhaps guarded by cross bunkers or humps which throw the ball to one side or the other.

The first famous hole is the 3rd, a par 5 of 482 yards (441 m) called the Cardinal. It takes its

RIGHT The clubhouse at Prestwick is a monument to Scottish solidity.

BELOW An example of the severe bunkering found at Prestwick. Note the sturdy timber supports typical of the course.

name from the huge timber-supported cross bunkers. These once had to be carried with, say, a brassie second; today they are hardly in play for long hitters who are firing their seconds over the angle of the dogleg directly for the green. The 5th includes the Himalayas, a range of dunes which have to be carried en route to the green of this par 3 of just over 200 yards (185 m). The conclusion of the first half lies on flatter land more away from the sea, but the 7th, 8th and 9th are all stiff par 4s of well over 400 yards (365 m). The course then heads back to the sea and dunes, much of it being set on land occupied by the original 12 holes. The 13th is a very difficult hole, at 460 yards (420 m) with a green set in typical links humps and hollows and at an angle to the line of shot.

A classic example of an 'old-fashioned' hole is still to come. This is the 17th, just under 400 yards (365 m) long. Here the second shot is blind over dunes known as the Alps, and the green beyond is then protected by a large cross bunker. In times past, one of the thrills of golf was to hit a blind shot and then, perhaps at the run, hurry to see the result; on the Alps hole, the question is will the ball be nestling close to the flag or buried in the cross bunker?

More Open Championships had been held at Prestwick than anywhere else until St Andrews caught up in 1984. Muirfield, with 13, comes next. Young Tom Morris had four victories here, and Harry Vardon three.

RIVIERA

RIVIERA COUNTRY CLUB
BEVERLY HILLS
LOS ANGELES
CALIFORNIA
UNITED STATES

RIGHT The crowds mass in this natural amphitheatre, which offers spectators a panoramic view of tournament play.

Designed by George Thomas in the mid-1920s, Riviera saw some of Ben Hogan's greatest feats, so much so that the professionals and the press began to call it 'Hogan's Alley'. In 1947 and 1948 he won the Los Angeles Open here and in the latter year also the first of his four US Open titles. Jimmy Demaret broke the US Open record by three strokes with his 278, but Hogan's response was to go two better! It was his third win at Riviera in under 18 months.

Even so, a perhaps greater achievement lay ahead. Early in 1949, Hogan was grievously injured in a car crash. Not long after he had managed merely to walk a golf course once again, Hogan entered the 1950 Los Angeles Open. He wondered if he could possibly manage to play 72 holes of golf. In the event, he tied for first place, later losing the play-off to Sam Snead.

Hogan was still not done with Riviera. After his amazing comeback, Hollywood thought him a fit subject for the first (and still the only) golfing epic movie. *Follow the Sun* (1951) was largely shot at Riviera with Hogan watching every move and apparently causing both director (Sidney Lanfield) and star (Glenn Ford) some pain because of his insistence on accuracy and attention to points of detail. This has not been Riviera's only contact with the movie industry: many stars and other film people have been members. Another – totally unrelated – aspect of the glamour of the place is that the equestrian events of the 1932 Olympics were held here.

The course has two dominant features. One is a gully that comes into play on eight of the holes and the other is Kikuyu grass. This was imported to stop erosion in the gully when flash floods occurred. It did the job successfully, but it also spread all over the course. The result is unusual. Balls pitching into this erect grass in the semi-rough and even on the fairways tend to bounce upward rather than onward, so that a running approach is impossible to predict.

The course begins with the easiest hole, a par 5 downhill of about 500 yards (460 m). Birdies are not easy to come by on the 2nd, however, which is uphill and swinging to the right. It was Hogan's favourite hole. What he thought of an oddity at the short 6th is not recorded. There is a bunker actually *in* the green and club players are not allowed to chip over it, a local rule which seems hard to defend. Perhaps George Thomas, if indeed it was he who was responsible, was thinking of one of the greens at North Berwick in Scotland, which has a mini-ravine running through it!

ABOVE Ben Hogan pictured in 1948, the year he won the US Open at Riviera.

ABOVE RIGHT George Thomas designed the course at Riviera in one of the golden ages of golf expansion – the 1920s.

RIGHT Ben Hogan (left), his wife Valerie and Glenn Ford, who played Hogan in *Follow the Sun*, the film of the golfer's epic struggle for fitness and renewed success following his devastating car accident.

ROYAL DORNOCH

ROYAL DORNOCH
GOLF CLUB
DORNOCH, SUTHERLAND
SCOTLAND

'About this town along the sea coast are the fairest and largest links or green fields of any pairt of Scotland. Fitt for archery, golfing, ryding and all other exercises, they doe surpass the fields of Montrose or St Andrews.' So wrote Sir Robert Gordon in 1630. There is an even earlier reference to golf being played near this little cathedral town. In 1616 it was noted in account books that the Earl of Sutherland had spent money on archery and golf clubs and balls while a schoolboy in the town. The only earlier references to golf links in Scotland are in connection with St Andrews and Leith, both from the preceding century. No one knows precisely when the game was first played at such famous places as St Andrews, Dornoch, Leith, Montrose, Gullane, Musselburgh and so on: all we have are the first handwritten or printed records. So it is just possible that Dornoch is the oldest golfing territory in the world.

After this early reference, Dornoch drifted out of golf history for many years, although there is no reason to doubt that golfers continued to play the links. More activity came in the mid-19th century, although it was still some time before a formal club was established, in 1877. By 1886, after two visits from St Andrews by Old Tom Morris, the club had an 18-hole course.

Famous golfers soon began to come – J H Taylor, Harry Vardon, James Braid, Horace Hutchinson and Walter Travis, for example. However, it was perhaps the spectacular achievements of the English amateur Joyce Wethered, often said to have learned the game during summer holidays here, that brought the Dornoch name to a wider public. This was in the early 1920s, when the course became very popular with summer visitors, some of whom were among the best amateur golfers of their day. Since then, the course has been very highly rated by the US golf writer Herbert Warren Wind and by Ben Crenshaw and Tom Watson, among others.

The rating of golf courses is a matter of taste, but certainly Dornoch is one of the world's great links courses. Many enthusiasts would claim it as the best in the British Isles. But, like the Royal North Devon at Westward Ho!, Dornoch is remote – 50 miles (80 km) beyond Inverness.

Unfortunately this has deterred many major events from coming here, including, of course, the Open Championship.

The course has a traditional out-and-back layout, the first eight holes running between due north and northeast. These holes are on a higher level, the tee shot on the 8th having a steep fall in the fairway down to almost beach level. The 9th, 10th, 11th, 12th, 13th, 15th and 16th all play close by the shore, and the others are only a little inland.

The 1st hole is a short par 4, a gentle introduction; but the 2nd, a 180-yard (165-m) par 3, features one of the typical Dornoch plateau greens: there are steep falls to either side. The 5th is the first classic hole: at about 360 yards (330 m), not a long par 4. There is a high tee but a mound to be carried 150 yards (137 m) or so away with bunkers to the right and, to the left, the gorse-covered hillside. The plateau green is quite long but narrow and well protected.

The 6th, a par 3 of 165 yards (151 m), is easy enough – if you hit and hold the green. Otherwise, all kinds of perils lie in wait. The 8th is a very attractive hole, nearly 440 yards (400 m) long, with a steep downslope in the fairway about 200 yards (180 m) or so out which rewards a good drive. The second shot at this hole must avoid bumpy ground and bunkers to find a receptive green in a dell.

The journey home begins with a 500-yard (460-m) par 5 all along the shore to a plateau green. This is the first of only two par 5s. All told, Dornoch is not particularly long, at just under 6,600 yards (6,035 m). It is the par 4s that make it the test it is, nine of them being over 400 yards (365 m). Perhaps the most difficult is the 14th, at about 450 yards (410 m), a hole Harry Vardon greatly admired. It is the only one on the course without a bunker, but there are other problems to compensate. The second shot needs to be very good. Again there is a plateau green with a steep rise up to it. Fingers of higher ground protect the right-hand side of the green. It all makes for a very difficult target, so a long drive is necessary if you are to be able to ease the shot in.

The 15th, only some 320 yards (290 m) long, provides respite, especially if you have been

battling home against the wind. The last three holes are all par 4s of over 400 yards (365 m), with the 17th being the pick. There is a downhill tee shot and then, a little less than 200 yards (180 m) out, the fairway has a step of nearly 50 feet (15 m). The hole then swings quite sharply left toward the plateau green, set well above the fairway and guarded by bunkers left and right. Unusually, this hole plays away from the club-house, going northward like the first eight holes. The final hole is over 450 yards (410 m) and very testing for second shots. There are bunkers about 30 yards (27 m) before the green, and then a grassy swale just short of it which stops many a shot from reaching the green.

At Dornoch the weather can change the course utterly. I remember two consecutive days I spent there one spring. The first was dominated by a howling snowstorm, and I saw just two lone Americans on the course – they had come a long way and they were not going to let a little thing like a blizzard deter them! I was out at dawn the following day. The sun shone and there might have been just a breath of wind.

ABOVE Dornoch is played on two levels – note the step in the fairway at the 17th hole.

LEFT Peter Alliss driving along the shoreline at dawn on a rare calm day at Dornoch.

ROYAL MELBOURNE WEST

ROYAL MELBOURNE
GOLF CLUB
SANDRINGHAM
MELBOURNE, VICTORIA
AUSTRALIA

There are two splendid courses of tournament calibre at Royal Melbourne, the East and the West. Alister Mackenzie was commissioned to design the West in 1926. He took a former Australian Open Champion, Alex Russell, into partnership for the work, and in fact it was Russell who produced the East a few years later. For major events, a composite of the two courses is used, partly to help handle large crowds and partly to avoid too many road crossings.

At the time, Alister Mackenzie was probably the most celebrated architect in the world and his work was international. In his native British Isles opportunities to work with really good golfing country had become limited: much had been used already and the Depression of the 1930s would lead to a farther decline in golf-course development. Mackenzie did most of his work in the United States, where his reputation today rests on Cypress Point and Augusta National. His Australian masterpiece is the West Course at Royal Melbourne. No other architect has such a trio of great courses to his credit. His fee for this one was 1,000 guineas (£1,050), quite a large sum for the time but hardly comparable with the hundreds of thousands of dollars a number of top architects can command today.

Although the 1st is of quite a stiff length for an opening hole, a par 4 of just under 430 yards (395 m), the fairway is almost as unmissable as on the 1st at St Andrews. The second shot, most unusually for this course, is not threatened by severe greenside and approach bunkering. However, once you are on the green, you soon become aware of one of the things that Royal Melbourne is all about: although very true, it is as fast as you will find anywhere in the world, and this means that any shot to the green that finishes far from the hole will often lead to three putts before being holed.

The 2nd, a short par 5 at only 480 yards (440 m), rewards a bold tee shot. If you carry an array of bunkers at about 200 yards (180 m), a near dogleg is straightened out and the green is reachable with a second shot by a reasonable hitter. Even so, there is a crater left of the green and other bunkers to the right. The 3rd, from the championship tees, is little more than 350 yards (320 m) in length, but the green slopes away

and so the pitch must be struck with plenty of bite.

So far, the course has made no demands for long hitting, but this changes with a vengeance at the 4th, a 470-yard (430-m) par 4 for tournament players (it is a more kindly par 5 for members and visitors). For the tee shot, there is the typical Mackenzie hazard of an upslope set with bunkers. There is rough short of the green, so the second shot must carry all the way.

There follow two of the best golf holes in Australia. The first of these is a par 3 of 170 yards (155 m) or so. It is played from a high tee to an elevated green, with almost continuous bunkers to the right and more of the same to the left. The straightest of shots will not be enough unless you judge the distance just as precisely. The green slopes markedly from the rear to the front, with quite a steep slope leading up to the green. The 'safe' shot well past the flag makes three putts more than likely, and the iron shot that just reaches the green will probably drift back down the green and then the slope, so that you have to make a short pitch to get back again.

The 6th, at about 430 yards (395 m), is a dogleg right from a high tee. This gives you the option of attempting to carry across the angle in order to shorten the second shot to the green. The shorter the better, in fact, because the bunkering on the left is very deep. The slope up to the green gives problems similar to those of the previous hole.

The next classic hole is the 10th, a par 4 of little more than 300 yards (275 m). As it is a dogleg left, a carry of about 250 yards (230 m) will find the green. However, the angle is defended by a vast, deep bunker. Long hitters must choose between the chance of a 2 if successful or a likely 5 if they fail by the merest scintilla. There are no such options on the next two holes, which are both long and tough par 4s. Then comes a lull for three holes, where not too much should go wrong, before that essential of the championship course – a stern finish. The 16th is a long par 3 of nearly 220 yards (200 m) to an island green surrounded by sand, while the 17th also requires a long second shot to the green – which can be fiendishly difficult to putt. At the

LEFT Many players have praised Alister Mackenzie's Australian masterpiece at Royal Melbourne. Note the gentle downhill approach to the green.

last hole, the shot to the green is relatively undramatic; bunkers abound, but they appear to be set to trap the poor shot rather than the one that is not quite good enough, and the green itself is of very generous size. But the tee shot is another matter entirely. Alister Mackenzie produced one of his favourite situations for the golfer, a blind tee shot over a well bunkered slope – and on this one he excelled himself. The slope is almost wholly sand, the tongues of grass that finger their way into the hazard offering menace, not relief.

Many great players have heaped praise on Royal Melbourne. Lee Trevino was particularly eloquent in the mid-1970s. He departed vowing never to return, more than a little piqued, perhaps, by a 9 on one hole. Earlier, he had thought it the best course in the world!

ROYAL RABAT

ROYAL GOLF
DAR-ES-SALAAM
RABAT
MOROCCO

At one time the present British royal family were quite enthusiastic golfers. King Edward VII started the trend: he used to play at Cannes, had a golf course laid out in the grounds of Windsor Castle and granted a number of golf clubs the right to the 'Royal' prefix. However, King Edward was hampered in developing his golf game by his enormous girth. Two of his sons, however, Edward VIII and George VI were medium-handicap players, but over the past 40 years, the interest of leading members of the House of Windsor seems to have lapsed. Two kings of Belgium, however, have been much better players of a very good amateur standard but perhaps King Hassan II of Morocco has outstripped them all, in enthusiasm if not playing skill. One result of this encouragement is the measure of popularity of golf in the country; although perhaps the first enthusiast was Haj Glaoui, Pasha of Marrakesh, where golf was certainly established by 1923.

Royal Rabat, one of Robert Trent Jones's monster designs, was opened at the beginning of the 1970s. There are now three courses but the great course is the Red, which can be stretched to about 7,500 yards (6,860 m). At this length it is almost impossible to score well as there is little run to be had on the soft, sandy soil. Royal Rabat is, in fact, shortened even for tournament play and was cut to about 7,200 yards

(6,585 m) for the 1987 Moroccan Open which began the year's European Tour. Howard Clark won with a winning score of 284, a high figure for a modern tournament. Even so, he needed a course record of 66 to help him to that total. He had no other round less than 72.

For general play, however, Royal Rabat is shortened and is a pleasure to play. The course is very well maintained with a staff said to number no fewer than 200! The greens are especially good, very fast but equally true. Long, straight tee shots are essential, for the course was basically cut through a forest of cork oak. Even if the player gets both length and direction, however, the subtly sloping fairways tend to direct many good shots into flanking bunkers.

Water, with flamingoes and duck, is often in sight, particularly at the most famous hole, the short 9th – still 199 yards (180 m) from the back tee. Here there is a lake to carry all the way to the green. A good professional once failed to make the shot six times. A lake is once again a threat on perhaps the most difficult hole on the course, the 11th, a par 4 of nearly 465 yards (425 m). Any shot wandering left will find water and then, faced with at least a long iron in, the green is tiny at only about 12 yards (11 m) from front to back. Most of the greens are far larger but you will then notice one of Jones's trade marks – severe contouring. Your approach shot needs to be quite near the hole to avoid 3-putting.

Even if the round has been a disaster from beginning to end, there are still two consolations. The setting is beautiful and the green fees low.

BELOW This walkway crosses a stretch of water to what is virtually an island green at Royal Dar es Salaam.

ROYAL ST GEORGE'S

ROYAL ST GEORGE'S
GOLF CLUB
SANDWICH, KENT
ENGLAND

Dr Laidlaw Purves was one of the most opinionated gentlemen any golf club has had to suffer among its members. His main club was Royal Wimbledon, which he joined in 1874. Within 10 years he was on the committee, but shortly afterward he resigned. Why? His daughter gave a clue when she noted that, although he had a heart of gold, he was 'the most irascible man I ever met'.

Even so, Purves was chosen captain of the club and busied himself at various times trying to unify the rules of golf (his club used a 3-inch [7.5-cm] hole in the mid-1870s while a 4¼-inch [11-cm] one was in use at St Andrews!), produced a logical handicapping system, and sent a constant stream of suggestions to the committee – all of which were ignored. The doctor is still remembered at Royal Wimbledon but his wider renown comes from his connections with Royal St George's.

Golf on Wimbledon Common was poor stuff, as on so many London courses not in the heathland belt. Purves and others were on the lookout for choicer land, perhaps mainly for weekend and holiday golf. One day in 1887 he came down to the little medieval town of Sandwich and went up the tower of the Norman church to inspect the view. What he saw excited him – a superb stretch of dunes, linksland and saltmarsh, which would many years later become not one but three courses: the Royal Cinque Ports at Deal, Prince's, and Royal St George's. Purves quickly formed the Sandwich Bay Golfing Association and we can be sure they were soon playing golf: in those times the leading lights of a club rapidly decided where the greens should be, and play began almost the next day.

Dr Purves is still credited as designer of the course, although some say that the first professional must have been closely involved. This is not necessarily so. Purves had designed a course for the ladies at Wimbledon and was later much annoyed when his plans for a new men's course were rejected by the committee. If he was in control, as at Sandwich, no one else would have been given much chance to argue a case.

The new club and course very quickly became

popular with those eager to play golf away from the soggy clays of the London area. Soon it won wider recognition, the Amateur Championship coming to it just five years after the club was formed. A few years later the same championship was played here again. In between, something even more momentous happened: in 1894 the first Open Championship to be held outside Scotland was at Sandwich. (It was won by an Englishman, J H Taylor.)

There have been several other 'firsts'. In 1904 the Amateur Championship passed out of UK hands for the first time, being won by Walter Travis, an Australian-born American. More momentous events came to the area in the early 1920s. Walter Hagen turned up to play at neighbouring Deal expecting to win. He was 53rd. Two years later, at Sandwich, Hagen became the first US-born Open Champion. Of his four Open victories, the third also came at Sandwich, in 1928. Hagen's wins were part of a long string of US successes in the British Open. This was unbroken between 1924 and 1934, when probably the greatest UK golfer of all time, Henry Cotton,

ABOVE The starters' hut and 1st tee at Royal St George's with the clubhouse in the background.

ABOVE Dr Laidlaw Purves discovered the golfing land at Sandwich.

ABOVE The US golfer Walter Travis in play during the 1904 Amateur Championship at Royal St George's.

won his first Open – again at Royal St George's.

The Open continued to come periodically to this corner of Kent until 1949, when attendances were very poor, so that the R & A dropped the course from the rota. There were many things against it, including notably a little toll bridge that caused traffic hold-ups any day of the week. For more than 30 years the course stayed off the rota: what chaos might ensue now that the Open Championship had become big business? Nevertheless, in 1981 the time was judged right for a return; Bill Rogers won and has scarcely been heard from since. In 1985 at Sandwich Sandy Lyle became the first UK winner since Tony Jacklin in 1969.

Despite its high rate of usage today, the 'St Andrews of the South' is less popular with professionals, US professionals especially. The main reason is the high number of blind shots. Modern professionals do not mind the occasional blind drive, but they do like to be able to see the bottom of the flag for the shots to the green. For these and other reasons, many think that Royal St George's is the most difficult of the courses

ABOVE This Harry Rountree painting, dated c 1910, amply illustrates the wild links terrain.

used for the Open. In 1985, Jack Nicklaus missed the 36-hole cut for the first time ever, and earlier, in 1981, he had an 83 in his first round before fighting back magnificently with a 66. The winning scores likewise illustrate the difficulties of the course. In 1981 Bill Rogers was four under par at the finish; the runner-up, Bernhard Langer, equalled par, and the men in third place were three over. When Lyle won, he was two over. The course length is just over 6,800 yards (6,220 m), playing to a par of 70.

Royal St George's gives a splendid sense of space, every hole being entirely separate. (Within the course boundaries there is just about enough spare land to lay out another course!) Although the player does not return to the vicinity of the clubhouse until the 18th, this is by no means the traditional Scottish out-and-back links lay-out. There are many changes of direction, so that a wind will come at a player from every direction during the course of a round. A good score often needs to be made on the first nine, mainly because you are unlikely to pick up shots

during the stern finish from the 13th onwards.

Even so, the start can be just as daunting. The 1st, over 440 yards (400 m) long, has an invitingly wide fairway, but the green is unreachable into a wind. The par-3 3rd, well over 200 yards (180 m), has an upslope to the green and often requires a wooden club shot. The 4th, at 466 yards (426 m), is one of the longest of the par 4s and a right-to-left dogleg. Bunkers on the right threaten shorter hitters, and there are more on the left at the angle of the dogleg. The 5th is another long 4, but from here on several of the holes until you reach the hard finish offer you some chance to improve the look of your scorecard.

Many think the 13th, a par 4 of length about 440 yards (400 m), the most difficult hole to par on the course, and the 14th, although not a long par 5 at just over 500 yards (460 m), is menaced by an out-of-bounds region along the right. There is the risk here that you can hit a good straight drive and then watch as your ball catches the side of a hump and bounds almost at right angles off the course. The hole takes its name,

Suez Canal, from a ditch which crosses the fairway 300 yards (275 m) or so from the tee. In fact, it should not be in play provided your drive has been a reasonable one.

At the 15th a good drive is needed to reach the fairway – but then this is true of Sandwich as a whole: it is no place for a golfer used to getting away with topping the occasional tee shot. Just short of the green on the 15th are three deep cross bunkers. The 16th is a good short par 3, certainly no monster at 165 yards (151 m), but heavily bunkered both in front and to either side. The 17th has one of the humpiest of the fairways. It is a good idea to err on the side of strength with your second shot, for the raised back of the green will very likely help the ball back on.

The last, a par 4 of nearly 460 yards (420 m), has settled a few big events. The professionals have been known to complain that they are expected to hold with a long iron a green that was originally designed to hold a more lofted shot. But there is a way to play it. The drive should be along the left; should you still need a long iron for the second, the shot should be a low runner.

In severe weather, when the rough is dense, Royal St George's is almost unplayable for moderate club golfers. Given a fine summer's day and the larks flying, it is a golfing paradise.

LEFT Sandy Lyle, the Scottish golfer, holds the famous claret jug after winning the 1985 Open over the course. He is also wearing the Championship Belt, won outright by Young Tom Morris more than a century ago. It is now owned by the Royal and Ancient Golf Club of St Andrews.

LEFT The 16th green is a heavily bunkered par 3.

ST ANDREWS OLD

THE ROYAL AND ANCIENT GOLF CLUB ST ANDREWS FIFE, SCOTLAND

To many golfers who have played the Old Course at St Andrews, the only thing 'great' about it is its reputation. Some of the finest players of all time have been puzzled by this reputation – some even openly contemptuous. J H Taylor, who won two Opens on the course, still never came to admire it. Sam Snead, who won the 1946 Open here, wrote later that it seemed an abandoned sort of place: he thought the land worth nothing more than planting with beet. Bobby Jones, who first played the course as a teenager in 1921 and tore up his card in disgust during his third round in the Open, at the time felt 'puzzled dislike'. Later, however, he was to declare (perhaps a couple of championship victories at St Andrews helped): 'Truly, if I had to select one course on which to play the match of my life, I should select the Old Course.' As Robert Tyre Jones Jr may well have been the most intelligent of the great golfers, his opinion cannot be lightly dismissed.

Certainly, when you first arrive at St Andrews, you wonder what all the fuss is about. Many golfers are outright puzzled when they step towards the 1st tee. The old sandstone clubhouse of the Royal and Ancient Golf Club certainly looks historic enough, a potent symbol of golf's venerability and probably more photographed than any other single feature of the course. But what is this before us? Apparently a flat field making up the 1st and 18th holes, giving both of them unbunkered fairways of very generous width indeed. Two features are visible. A swale of no great depth in front of the 18th green (the legendary Valley of Sin), from which it looks easy enough to putt, and a little stream (the Swilcan Burn) which is in play only for a very poor tee shot on the 18th but is an obvious threat just short of the 1st green. Both are manifestly holes of no more than drive-and-pitch length, unless you are playing into the wind.

If we look at our score card, more oddities immediately appear. There are only a couple of par 3s and, although they are long ones, only a couple of par 5s. There is also a surprising sequence of four par 4s between the 7th and the 12th, all of which are well under 400 yards (365 m), a couple of which are surely drivable with a tail wind. (The 10th and 12th in fact are,

although you cannot have a following wind on both of them on the same day.)

And what of the feel of history? Golf has been played here for well over five and a half centuries, but there are no clear signs of this. That venerable clubhouse, built in 1854, is hardly an ancient monument. From the 1st tee you see a row of quaint shops to the left. But, further on, a few hundred yards away, is the Old Course Golf and Country Club. Some think it a hideous monstrosity, modern hotel architecture at its worst. This is to overstate things, but certainly the building does nothing to enhance the feeling that golf has been played here since the dawn of time – neither do a handful of modern houses the city fathers have allowed to be built close along the left.

Photographers know what is wanted. The sur-

LEFT A view of the town of St Andrews from the course.

BELOW LEFT The 19th-century clubhouse is the home of the R and A which, in partnership with the USGA, administers the rules of golf and independently organizes the British championships.

roundings you see in their pictures are the club-house, the edge of the town huddling close around the 18th green and the St Andrews sky-line viewed from out on the course. There is one truly venerable feature, a little stone bridge, several hundred years old, which crosses the Swilcan Burn on the 18th. In 1810, it was 'al-most impassable' and repairs were ordered to what was then known as the 'Golfer's Bridge'.

But enough of history: let us instead explore the course. At the 1st, the drive is almost too easy but, especially if the flag is to the front of the green, the second shot must be precisely weighted. It must, of course, clear the burn, but if it is only a little too strong you find yourself with a testing downhiller to the hole. The 2nd, at just over 400 yards (365 m), gives some clues as to how to play the Old Course. Almost invariably, the best line to ease the second shot is along the right of the fairway, as here, yet the safest line for the tee shot is usually very different — you have to drive to the left to make sure you stay clear of the worst trouble. This, of course, makes the second shot more difficult ... Because of this trait of the course Seve Ballesteros, in his plan to win the 1984 championship, adopted a simple philosophy — keep out of the bunkers. As long as he could do that from the tee, he was happy to accept more demanding shots to the green.

As early as this 2nd hole another feature of the course should become apparent. The ground in front of the greens is frequently undulating, and the humps and hollows often throw the ball off in unwelcome directions. The best shot to a green is almost always one which pitches on. This can be done in modern times, now that watering has made the greens far more holding than they used to be in dry weather. The practice started over 60 years ago, and has become increasingly used as time has gone by. Placement of the shot to the green, however, is still the main problem that prevents the stars returning lower scores than they do. Ballesteros thinks St Andrews the easiest of the British Open courses but a few statistics suggest he is wrong — or just personally lucky! To the end of 1983, for instance, there had been 22 rounds of between 63 and 65 in all of the British Opens. Only one of those was done at St Andrews; but in the 1980 championship alone, at Muirfield, there were three 64s and a 63!

The first really dramatic hole, as the course goes out over gently undulating ground, comes with the 5th, which has a steep fall down to the green. Golfers need to decide if their shots to the green at this par 5 should carry this feature or make use of it. Shortly after the 5th comes the famous 'loop', that sequence of two par 3s and four short par 4s. Most good scores for the round come from having a fair ration of 3s in this stretch. Only the 7th green, 372 yards (340 m) away with a bunker blocking the route to the flag, is not 'on' for the tee shot. However, do not take these comments to mean that you should regard these holes as easy meat. The par 3s, the 8th and 11th, can cause problems, especially the latter, a much imitated hole. The 9th, many think, is the worst on the course. It has a flat fairway and a green rather too like a tennis court. In the 1921 Open the champion, Jock Hutchison, holed the 8th in one and nearly repeated the feat on the 9th. Years later, Tony

Jacklin holed his second shot to the 9th in his first round of the 1970 championship to be out in 29.

After the 12th, there are certainly no more gift holes. The 13th is one of the great par 4s of world golf. There are the Coffin bunkers, apparently in the middle of the fairway, to avoid, and the shot to the green must be well struck to hold the putting surface, which slopes away from the player. The 14th is a perilous par 5, especially if there is a wind from your left blowing towards the out-of-bounds wall. The so-called Hell bunker used to be a terror for those trying to get up in two, but it is not quite as severe today. For good players, most problems come from playing the tee shot 'safely' to the left away from the out-of-bounds and instead finding the series of bunkers called the Beardies. The hole cost Gene Sarazen the title in 1933, and six years later Bobby Locke used up 15 strokes on it in his first two rounds. The 15th and 16th are both good par 4s, and some players lose concentration, thinking of the terrors immediately ahead. The 17th, a long par 4 at 461 yards (422 m), may be the most difficult hole in world golf. The safe way to play it is to drive left, play toward the front of the green, chip up to the pin and hope for a

ABOVE Bernhard Langer, the West German golfer, has never won the British Open Championship although he came close to winning the title here in 1984, finishing second.

much trouble. The second, depending on flag position, will either be a high pitch or a well weighted running approach, according to taste. In 1970, Doug Sanders needed a par 4 to win the Open. His drive was good but his second was too firm, leaving him with quite a long downhill putt. He was a little too cautious, finished short of the hole, and missed the next one. The following day Jack Nicklaus won the play-off. Ironically, Sanders birdied the hole this time – but so did Nicklaus, who was already a stroke ahead.

It is often said that no one 'designed' the Old Course, as if it were some kind of spontaneous miracle. Yet human hands and minds most certainly did play their part. Those who first played over the terrain made choices about which natural features – little hollows and plateaux – made interesting sites for greens. Basically, however, these early golfers thought out a route away from their start point and then back again. Over time, 22 holes evolved, the 11th and the 22nd being played only once each while the rest were played on both outward and inward journeys. Other early homes of golf played the number of holes that suited the terrain they played over. Leith Links and Musselburgh, at one extreme, had five holes, Montrose had 25, and Prestwick, a much later arrival as a golf course, in the mid-19th century, decided that 12 was about the right number. A momentous event in the history of golf came on 4 October 1764. It was decided by the Royal and Ancient Golf Club, then in existence for just 10 years, that the first four holes were rather short and easy, and so they decided that two much longer holes would be better. They thereby invented the 18-hole course.

At much the same time, the last major changes were made at St Andrews. As it was hazardous to have golfers playing to the same greens both out and back, the course and the greens were widened, so that there would be two widely separate flag positions on each green. Today, some of these monster greens occupy virtually the whole width of the course – the only single greens are on the 1st, 9th, 17th and 18th. The last of these was made in the 1880s, and since that time very few changes at all have been made.

A few back tees have been constructed, and people say that a bunker in the middle of the joint fairways of the 1st and 18th was filled in during 1914 but apart from that the course has been left untouched.

single putt. Bold play means going for the 4, however. This means driving blind over the outline of the former railway sheds on the right and hopefully not out of bounds. If the drive finishes just in bounds, the shot to the green then becomes more possible. A drive to the left, however, leaves the green at an angle to the line in, the famous Road bunker barring the way. A ball played with too much strength will very likely run through the green and out onto the road beyond, eventually coming to rest against a stone wall. It is unlikely that anyone has ever played this hole in level par for all four rounds of a championship. In 1984, it destroyed Tom Watson. Ironically, he had played a superb drive down the right, ideally tight by the out-of-bounds, but then he pushed his second onto the road. Seve Ballesteros, in contrast, played the hole the 'wrong way': well to the left in the rough, he played a brilliant – and lucky – second shot which held the green. Watson, close to the wall, could not get his third close, and his chance of the championship was gone. Ballesteros made doubly sure with a birdie on the last.

And so to the 18th. Here you can slice the ball right over the fence into 'the old grey town', but otherwise the tee shot should not give you too

SHINNECOCK HILLS

SHINNECOCK HILLS
GOLF CLUB
SOUTHAMPTON
LONG ISLAND
NEW YORK
UNITED STATES

RIGHT The 1986 US Open was hosted by Shinnecock Hills – the first time the championship has been held there since 1896.

This is a club whose history is filled with 'firsts', and it was also involved in a major 'second'. Three of the founders were on holiday at Biarritz and watched the Scottish professional Willie Dunn play a succession of shots over a ravine. Said one of the three, William K. Vanderbilt: 'Gentlemen, this beats rifle-shooting for distance and accuracy. It is a game I think might go in our country.'

He spoke more wisely than he knew. Golf since then has been, to understate matters, rather successful in the United States. The founders of Shinnecock Hills thought they had introduced the game to the country when they brought Dunn over to lay out 12 holes for them in 1891. Even though the 'Apple Tree Gang', with their St Andrews Golf Club, had got there a couple of years earlier, Shinnecock Hills was one of the five clubs which founded what was later to be called the United States Golf Association.

As noted, the club has enjoyed some undisputed 'firsts', however. Shinnecock Hills was the first US club to incorporate and, in only a few years, the first to have a membership waiting list. When they called in the well known architect Stanford White, he produced the United States's first proper clubhouse for them.

In 1896 the course, by then 18 holes, was the scene of both the US Amateur and Open championships. In the latter, there was trouble before the off. John Shippen and Oscar Bunn had entered; the former was part black, part American Indian, and the latter was full American Indian. Some of the emigré Scottish professionals who were competing objected, but they were thankfully overruled. Shippen might have won but for an 11 on one hole, and James Foulis became champion.

The Shinnecock Hills Club had a champion of its own, however. This was Beatrix Hoyt, who won three US Ladies' Championships in the years 1896–8 and then retired.

From this time, Shinnecock Hills, a very exclusive club, saw no more great events until 1986. Then the US Golf Association took the bold – even perhaps rash – decision to bring the US Open to the end of Long Island. The players were delighted with the course, which was stretched to just over 6,900 yards (6,310 m), but scoring was high in the cold, wind and rain of the first day – although scores tumbled later, three players coming in with 65s on the last day. Raymond Floyd's final-round 66 was enough to bring him the championship, however.

Although all traces of them are long gone, Willie Dunn's original 12 holes probably represented the first authentic golf-course design in the United States. The present course dates from 1931, when William Flynn and Dick Wilson produced a lay-out which makes good use of the prevailing wind, the long par 4s playing with it and the short ones against it. Fairways are well separated and undulating. The turf, although inland in type, is closer in texture to British links than at almost anywhere else in the United States. The rough is usually fierce, so straight driving is at a premium, and length too is needed to carry fairway crests.

The four par 3s are a strong feature at Shinnecock Hills, with the 2nd being a particularly severe test, especially so early in the round. It is some 220 yards (200 m) long and plays over a valley to a well bunkered green. Although the remaining three are far shorter, the 11th, at 160 yards (146 m), presents a small target, and the 17th is perhaps the most beautiful hole on the course; it is named the Eden, after the St Andrews hole in Scotland.

SHOAL CREEK

Alabama is very much off the beaten track for tournament play. When the Professional Golfers' Association (PGA) decided to stage their championship at Shoal Creek in 1984, this was the first time that any Tour event had been held in the state since the 1960s.

The course was a relatively new one, but had risen rapidly in esteem. The reason was, to put it succinctly, Jack Nicklaus. Hall Thompson, an Augusta member, had bought some land for a golf course and a select housing development some 25 miles (40 km) south of Birmingham and, looking for a course architect, was advised to try Nicklaus, who was then at an early stage in his career as a golf architect. It took Jack, after a first visit to the site in 1974, two weeks to decide whether or not he felt he could produce a course over the rocky, forested landscape.

The result contains some of his trademarks. Many of the shots are slightly downhill. The shot to the green always allows a clear view of the flag. Another feature is that the par 5s, all over 500 yards (460 m) long – the 6th, at 554 yards (507 m), is the longest – can be reached in two by tournament players, but demand a second shot of excellence. The 11th is a good example of this. Anything short to the left, right or front will find the shallow but broad creek; then there

are bunkers that will catch most shots that are not of the highest quality. At the 17th – 539 yards (493 m) – Shoal Creek itself is in play, broadened into a lake to the left of the green. At the right front, boulders were put in. Of course, these do not come into play, but the waterfall they create makes this the most photographed hole on the course.

On the whole, the par 4s are perhaps a more severe test. Eight of these are over 400 yards (365 m) long, of which four are around 450 yards (410 m). Only one par 4 is shorter than 400 yards, the 14th: at 380 yards (347 m), even that is scarcely of drive-and-pitch length, and there is a lake confronting the tee shot. Probably the most difficult, however, is the 4th, at 458 yards (419 m). There is not a single bunker on the hole. Instead, Nicklaus used a grassy hollow in front of the green, reckoning that good players would find sand easier to play from.

Some have found the par 3s a weakness. All are between 177 and 197 yards (162–180 m) and, because of the shape of the land, may need the same club.

During the 1984 PGA, however, the most noticeable feature of all was the rough. Although it was not deep, every shot that missed the fairway seemed to settle well down. The ball simply disappeared. Perhaps that was why only one long hitter, Seve Ballesteros, finished in the top five – and he was fifth. Those ahead of him – Calvin Peete, Gary Player, Lanny Wadkins and especially the champion, Lee Trevino – are more renowned for subtlety of play than for sheer strength.

Player started badly with a 74, but after the second round it seemed very possible he could become the oldest winner ever of a major championship. He birdied all four par 3s and had six more birdies to be round in 63. That tied him with Trevino and Wadkins. They were still the leaders after the third round, and a Player miracle seemed in prospect when he holed a putt of well over 30 yards (27 m) on the 9th in the last round. However, over the last nine it proved to be a battle between Trevino and Wadkins, everyone's money being on the 34-year-old rather than on Trevino, who was by 1984, at the age of 44, a part-time competitor. In the end, however, Trevino had his way, winning by four strokes from Wadkins and Player.

Lee Trevino's victory put him in the record books as the fourth oldest golfer ever to win one of the four majors.

LEFT Lee Trevino became the US PGA Champion on this course in 1984 when he, and most others, thought his career at the top was over. He was 44.

BELOW LEFT The 11th with its shored-up green is a relatively easy hole if you are content to pitch on in 3, but presents a challenge for long hitters trying to reach it in 2.

SOUTHERN HILLS

SOUTHERN HILLS
COUNTRY CLUB
TULSA, OKLAHOMA
UNITED STATES

BELOW RIGHT Hubert Green won the 1977 US Open on this course, despite a death threat.

Hubert Green was on the 10th hole at Southern Hills in his final round of the 1977 US Open, a championship he had led throughout, when the police received an anonymous death threat: Green was going to be murdered at the 15th. He himself was not informed for quite some time, but TV cameras were put to work scanning the crowd around the 15th green. Before he played the hole, however, Green was given the option of withdrawing, carrying on or requesting a suspension of play. He decided to continue, and fortunately nothing happened.

His greatest problem, in fact, came on the 18th, not the 15th. This is a difficult par 4 of over 450 yards (410 m) which doglegs to the right, with the fairway narrowed by ponds at the angle. The tee shot is downhill, but this does not make the hole any easier, because the second shot is to an elevated green from a downhill lie. When Green came to the hole he needed a bogey 5 to win. After being bunkered and in the rough, he only just made the green with his third shot, then left his approach putt by no means dead. Unlike his similar Masters experience the next year, Green got his 3-footer – and the championship.

Only Green and the second man home, Lou

Graham, were under par at the end of the championship, the main reason being the dense rough in which balls just a foot or so off the fairway settled out of sight in the Bermuda grass. Green is not a long hitter and neither is Graham, but both men are better than most at keeping the ball in play on the fairway. In a previous US Open, the 1958 champion Tommy Bolt pointed to his driver when asked what had won him the title. If only two scored below 280 in 1977, in 1958 just three managed to break 290.

In the mid-1930s, after the vast expansion of golf during the 1920s in the United States, many clubs were having to shut down as a result of the Depression. Southern Hills was one of few to be constructed during this period, the oil money of Tulsa being the benefactor. It was designed by Perry Maxwell, who had also created Prairie Dunes and been called in by Bobby Jones and Clifford Roberts to make changes to Alister Mackenzie's Augusta. At Augusta Maxwell moved the 10th green and transformed an ordinary hole into a magnificent one.

Most consider Southern Hills to be a similar triumph. The course is often rated the best in the central United States, but its name is misleading.

It is very flat indeed, the only real slope being up to the clubhouse, so that the 9th and 18th have uphill second shots and the 1st and 10th play downhill. For championship play, the 13th is probably the toughest hole, shortened to a very long par 4 of 470 yards (430 m), instead of the 550-yard (500-m) par 5 the members play. This change in length is mainly because the United States Golf Association (USGA) likes the Open courses to play to a par of 70. In tournaments short hitters face a blind second shot over ponds to the left and right front of the green. Unlike the 13th, the 5th remains a par 5, a true monster at nearly 600 yards (550 m), with a tightly bunkered green at the end of the trek.

Bunkers are another main test on the course. Professionals learn and follow their trade in coarse sand. Southern Hills has very fine river sand. The professionals are not used to it — especially not to finding completely buried lies! There are also the trees which line the fairways, completing the picture of a course where it is often fatal to miss a fairway, even by inches, while perfect positioning on the fairway is also essential if you are to set up your shot into the undulating, banked greens.

ABOVE The 4-par 12th at Southern Hills was much praised by Ben Hogan. A particularly challenging hole, the green is guarded by bunkers and a blind water hazard. (© TONY ROBERTS 1986)

SPYGLASS HILL

SPYGLASS HILL
GOLF CLUB
PEBBLE BEACH
CALIFORNIA
UNITED STATES

RIGHT The last 13 holes at Spyglass Hill run inland from the Monterey Peninsula through pine forest. This is the 16th which at 465 yards (425 m) is the longest par 4 of the course.

FAR RIGHT The first 4 holes are out in links territory. The shot to the 3rd green must be precise; miss and you are bound to find sand.

Most first holes give golfers a fairly gentle introduction to the rigours that may lie ahead, but the one at Spyglass is an exception. It is a massive par 5 of 600 yards (550 m), swinging from left to right and heading for the sea. Play used to be dominated by a lone pine in the centre of the fairway; it is said that Robert Trent Jones designed the hole with the tree as the focal point. The next four holes are as near as you get to links golf in the United States, and they are fearsome when the wind is up, even though each is a relatively short par 4 or par 3.

The remainder of the holes lie in pine parkland. There is water on several holes in this section of the course, although usually it presents a problem only if your shot is wayward. An exception is on the 11th, a par 5, where the shot to the green must carry over water.

Undoubtedly holes 2 to 5 are the ones which make the most impact, particularly on US players unused to links golf, but the 12th is as interesting as any, a par 3 of some 180 yards (165 m), modelled like so many on the Redan at North Berwick, Scotland. The green is set a little aslant the line of play, and the problems are increased by water to the left of the green. The 14th is a long double dogleg of some 550 yards (500 m),

but the 16th is probably the most difficult hole, at 460 yards (420 m) or so, doglegging to the right with an elevated green.

The name of the course derives from Robert Louis Stevenson's *Treasure Island*. Stevenson spent some time living in the Del Monte Forest and is thought to have derived some of the inspiration for the book from the Pacific vistas. Names from the book were given to some of the holes – Long John Silver, Treasure Island, Jim Hawkins and so on. The course opened for play early in 1966, and Bing Crosby immediately added it to the rota for his tournament. Professionals in the first years were highly critical of its condition. Although those difficulties belong to the past, it is still considered by many to be the most difficult of the three used for the tournament, the others, of course, being Cypress Point and Pebble Beach.

When Jack Nicklaus arrived to play here for the first time, Crosby bet him '5' that he could not par the course at his first attempt. 'Five dollars or five grand?' Nicklaus asked. They settled on $500, and Nicklaus played round in a 2-under-par 70. In the tournament itself, however, his score was 2 over, 74, but he was still good enough to go on to win.

SUN CITY

THE GARY PLAYER
COUNTRY CLUB
SUN CITY, PILANSBERG
BOPHUTHATSWANA
SOUTH AFRICA

RIGHT A panoramic view of the Gary Player Country Club in its breathtaking setting at Sun City.

Set on the floor of an extinct volcano, this course — usually known as Sun City rather than by its formal name — was cut out of thorn tree and bush in little more than a matter of months during the late 1970s. At times it can be like a cauldron, and it depends very much on sophisticated watering systems.

It was created by Ronald Kirby and Gary Player, and one of their prime aims was to preserve the integrity of the land as far as possible: very few trees were cut down. The course features multiple island tees, the use of which can affect the length of some of the holes by as much as 100 yards (90 m). At full stretch, it measures over 7,650 yards (7,000 m).

Sol Kerzner, the promoter of Sun City, well knew the value of tournament play, and the first was held here in 1979, when the course was barely yet fit for play. A little later Kerzner promoted the first-ever tournament to have a prize of $1 million; it was won by Johnny Miller. The drama lay mostly in the sudden-death play-off, which was one of the longest ever. Nine holes went by before Severiano Ballesteros three-putted to give Miller his victory.

In 1987 the diminutive Welsh golfer Ian Woosnam won the $1-million cheque — his eighth important tournament victory of the year. This brought his total winnings for 1987 to over £1 million, an all-time record for a single year and approaching twice as much as anyone else had achieved. However, huge purses are becoming ever more frequent in professional tournaments and the Sun City Challenge has lost some of its appeal in recent years.

TURNBERRY AILSA

RIGHT An aerial view of the famous lighthouse, a distinctive feature of Turnberry, and of some of the sea holes. The vast hotel can be seen in the background.

In 1977 Turnberry was almost at its easiest for the Open Championship. True, the course had been set up to be as tough as possible, but the hot dry summer of 1976 (the year when the UK Government appointed a Minister for Droughts!) had ensured that the rough was not punishing. Jack Nicklaus, despite driving none too well throughout, was able to card his lowest four-round total ever in a major championship, 269 – and even then he did not win. Tom Watson gave what history may well rank as his greatest performance to win a thrilling two-man encounter by a single stroke.

Mind you, the course was not as easy for the rest of the field. Only one other player, Hubert Green, beat par – and he was 10 strokes behind the leaders. One rising star found it very difficult. He was a young Australian aged 22 who already had two tournaments to his credit: in Australia he had won the 1976 Westlakes Classic and in Great Britain the 1977 Martini. His name? Yes, you probably guessed it – Greg Norman. At Turnberry in 1977 there were two cuts. Norman just scraped through the 36-hole one with rounds of 78 and 72, but he was gone after 54 holes.

It was a very different story in 1986. The R & A seemed to want to make sure that no one humiliated Turnberry. The fairways were narrowed to about 25 yards (23 m). There were only a couple of yards of semi-rough before the knee-high stuff began.

As usual, Seve Ballesteros started as favourite. He thought the champion might come home at about 5 under. That was before the weather worsened. On the first day 80s were commonplace. Anyone with a 75 or better felt he had acquitted himself well. In the very stiff wind no one finished under par, and just one player, Ian Woosnam, was round in 70 to equal it. In much better weather (cloudy and chilly!) on the second day, Greg Norman played one of the great rounds of major championship history and matched the lowest round ever shot in the British Open, a 63 by Mark Hayes in the previous Turnberry Open. Norman birdied the 2nd, 3rd and 4th and followed this up with an eagle on the 7th. He was out in a 32 which included two bogeys. On the second nine he piled up five more birdies and then – an anticlimax if ever there was one – three-putted the last for his 63. That round brought him from 4 behind to a 2-stroke lead. By the end of the championship, Norman was a commanding 5 ahead and the only man to equal par for 72 holes.

But this was Turnberry in severe weather and set up to examine the best. For the visiting golfer on a reasonable day there are many more difficult courses. However, there are few that are more exhilarating.

Turnberry has a curious history. It was first laid out by a former Open Champion, Willie Fernie, early in this century as part of what is claimed to have been the first hotel-and-golf-course centre in the world. Like the very different Gleneagles, it proved very popular until World War II came. It

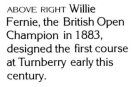

ABOVE RIGHT Willie Fernie, the British Open Champion in 1883, designed the first course at Turnberry early this century.

then became an RAF Coastal Command training airfield. Although the cause was clearly a very good one, surely no other championship course – certainly in the British Isles – has been so devastated. The characteristic sand dunes had to be levelled, bunkers were filled in, and much of the Ailsa and Arran courses was covered by concrete runways. Some of those runways still remain, although off either course, but an occasional out-of-bounds drive can bound, skip and run for hundreds of yards along what has become a parking area for spectators' cars.

After the war, it was found that detailed drawings and models had survived, and Philip Mackenzie Ross used these as a basis for recreating Turnberry Ailsa and Arran. Although the Ailsa course is much longer and is the one used

for big events, the Arran is well worth playing and is perhaps a better test of straight driving.

Ailsa begins with a series of unspectacular par 4s, though the 3rd, at 475 yards (434 m) from the championship tees, can be very difficult. The stretch that most remember best, however, is that from the 4th to the 11th, running close alongside the sea. The 4th is a par 3 which looks more difficult than it really is, with a green cut into the side of a dune and much peril if you miss on the left. The 5th is a scenic hole, a fairly short par 5, played from a high tee to a valley with dunes on either side before it doglegs left. The 6th, a long par 3 of over 240 yards (220 m), again looks more difficult than it is, unless the player is in a cavernous bunker in the upslope towards the green. With the wind behind you it

ABOVE A view down the 18th towards the green photographed in a brief spell of sunshine during the 1986 Open.

can be little more than a mid-iron shot, but it is impossible for almost anyone to reach when the wind is against. The 7th is another fine hole, and can be played as a par 4 or a 5; it doglegs left to follow the shoreline. As a par 4, it is probably the toughest hole on the course, with the ground rising to the green.

The most spectacular tee shot comes at the 9th. Championship competitors retire to a tee set on a rocky promontory and require a carry of 200 yards (180 m) to reach the fairway across an inlet. However, this is nothing like the 16th at Cypress Point. Few professionals fail to make the carry, but they tend to complain when they produce a perfect tee shot only to find that their ball has kicked away into the semi-rough. During the 1986 Open, Jack Nicklaus enquired if anyone had managed to stay on the fairway here! And staying on is important at this hole

because there is a long second shot to play.

As Turnberry Ailsa is an out-and-back lay-out, if the long 4s on the first nine have been almost impossible because of a wind from the north, relief comes on the inward half, which is also about 200 yards (180 m) shorter. The golf is less exhilarating, however – although still good enough for most. The 15th, at its full length of about 220 yards (200 m), is a very difficult par 3. It was very influential in helping Tom Watson win the 1977 Open when he holed a vast putt from well off the green to draw level with Nicklaus, who had played much the better tee shot but came away with a 3 to Watson's 2.

Although streams are not a major Turnberry feature, the broad one which crosses the fairway just short of the 16th green certainly is. Because the banks slope gently, there is little chance of an approach shot bounding across. To judge by

Jack Nicklaus and Tom Watson take a break during the 1977 Open. Following an epic contest between these two players, Watson finally emerged the champion – his second of five British Open victories.

RIGHT Greg Norman on his way to victory in the 1986 Open. This was to be his first major championship win.

its length, it is a potential birdie hole, but most golfers choose to play well toward the back of the green so that their shot does not spin back into the stream.

With the wind behind, the par-5 17th can be a question of a drive followed by a 6- or 7-iron shot for professionals. Club golfers who dare to give their drive everything from the high tee should be able to get home with a wood second shot.

The par-4 18th, lengthened for championship play to 430 yards (393 m), is the hole which Tom Watson played to perfection to hold onto his 1-stroke lead in 1977. He banged a 2-iron down the middle and then hit a mid-iron to about two feet (60 cm) of the hole. He needed to. Nicklaus, after sending his drive almost into the bushes along the right, holed a vast birdie putt.

WESTWARD HO!

ROYAL NORTH DEVON
GOLF CLUB
WESTWARD HO!, DEVON
ENGLAND

BELOW Spectators gather for an important match around the turn of the century. Note the boy caddies.

This club is the oldest in England still playing over its original ground, in this case Northam Burrows. Golf had been played earlier elsewhere in England. Blackheath claims to have been in existence since 1608, although there is no written proof for this, and certainly goes back as far as 1766. Old Manchester was formed in 1818 and played over Kersal Moor. However, in neither of these cases do the clubs still play over their original courses.

It is likely that Scottish influence brought golf to the northwest and northeast of England before the game began to be played over Northam Burrows. There is the definite example of Old Manchester, and a club was formed at Alnmouth, Northumberland, in 1869. However, there are stories that seafarers from Holland brought a version of the game to the flat linksland by the village of Alnmouth considerably earlier, although no one knows precisely when this might have been.

The history of the Royal North Devon and golf played there even before the club's foundation in 1864 is well documented. It all began with two men, General Moncrieff and William Driscoll Gossett. They visited the Rev. I. H. Gossett at Westward Ho! and both thought that the Burrows would be suited to golf. The general went so far as to declare: 'Providence evidently intended this for a golf links.'

Casual play began in 1853, but activity was spasmodic for a few years. In 1860, however, Old Tom Morris came down from Prestwick before the first Open Championship, stayed for a month and rearranged the course. He returned in the year of the club's foundation for a week or so and very likely suggested further changes. At this time, the idea that a golf course should necessarily consist of 18 holes was still some way off. The North Devon and West of England Golf Club (its first name) gave the golfer a choice between 17 and 22 holes: if you wanted to play a 'short' round, you just missed out the 13th to the 17th.

In 1867 the club gained royal approval and its present name, and in the following year the Westward Ho! and North Devon Ladies' Club was formed, believed to be the first for women in the British Isles. There was a rule that read: 'No other club shall on any account be used on the

Ladies' Course but a wooden putter.' This was probably because it was felt unladylike to raise a club above shoulder level.

The Royal North Devon rapidly became famous. It was particularly popular with golfers from Blackheath and Wimbledon. The land they played over at home was poor stuff for golf, and Westward Ho! gave them the real thing. As Bernard Darwin later wrote: 'To go to Westward Ho! is not to make a mere visit of pleasure as to an ordinary course; it is a reverent pilgrimage.' He added: 'It is a splendid course, not only wonderfully difficult and wonderfully interesting but it has a charm given to few links. It looks more like a good golf course than almost any other in the world.' The great golf architect Herbert Fowler, who made considerable changes at Westward Ho! early this century, was referring to Prestwick, Royal St George's and Muirfield when he wrote: 'None of these courses can compare with Westward Ho! as a test of the highest form of golf and the only reason ever given why championships are not played there is that it is out of the way.' Perhaps the last word should be left with J H Taylor. He thought it simply 'the finest natural links in the world'.

Yet no Open Championships have come to Westward Ho! Perhaps the most likely time would have been, say, between the 1880s and the start of World War I. But, as Fowler noted, it *is* out of the way and so the Royal North Devon's course does not have the fame of places where the great events have been played (although both the Amateur Championship and professional tournaments have come). Travel has become far easier, but Westward Ho! is still rather far from the major population centres which are necessary if a really big event is to be staged. Maybe an act of faith is needed: the R & A acted on one when they first chose Turnberry in 1977, and again when they risked road problems when they took the Open back to Sandwich in 1981 after a gap of over 30 years.

The start is not promising. The opening and finishing holes are flat – if not as flat as they look – and the Burrows only begin with the 3rd. The 4th, at 354 yards (324 m), has a famous hazard, a vast cross bunker that must be carried from the tee. The face is timbered, and there is a local rule which allows a player within two club-lengths a free drop the same distance further back.

A much more unusual local rule concerns the 'Great Sea Rushes'. These are a unique and very sharply pointed feature of the course. If you get

ABOVE In trouble in the Great Sea Rushes, this traditionalist is using hickory shafts to extricate himself from this hazard unique to Westward Ho!

in them, you can declare your ball lost and drop another for a penalty of only one stroke (rather than stroke and distance) near the point of entry. These rushes are most in play on the 10th, 11th and 12th, where they have to be carried from the tee, and there are other points where they can be seen – but preferably not entered.

All the middle section of the course is played among the sand dunes of the Burrows and, as Taylor said, looks entirely natural. Fowler's work was so in keeping with the terrain that players of today tend to believe that nothing has been altered at Westward Ho! since golf began there. The arrival of the rubber core ball meant changes everywhere, however, except at the Old Course, St Andrews, which was perhaps too long for gutta percha.

Although many have thought it unfortunate, the clubhouse is not down by the sea among the dunes; its situation inland is responsible for the flatness of the first and final holes. Still, even this can help the sense of anticipation. The golfer starts off in a dull landscape, but the promised land lies ahead ... At the flat finish, the stream which runs across short of the final green has settled many a match. Then comes the clubhouse, which contains many memories of Royal North Devon's history. A museum was opened in 1985 and rehoused in a separate building during 1987.

WINGED FOOT WEST

WINGED FOOT GOLF CLUB
MAMARONEK
WESTCHESTER COUNTY
NEW YORK
UNITED STATES

The toughest holes in golf are those that demand long shots to the greens. These holes are not the apparently daunting par 5s – of, say, 550 yards (500 m) – but long par 3s and 4s that demand long irons and woods for the shots in. The difficulties of the West Course at Winged Foot derive from the long par 4s. When the course is set up for championship play, there are 10 over 400 yards (365 m) long – and most of them considerably longer. The members have it slightly easier, for two of these holes revert to not particularly long par 5s for normal play. Over 60 years ago, they asked their chosen architect, A W Tillinghast, for 'a man-sized course' . . . and that is what they certainly got. The East Course is almost as good.

Tillinghast was presented with heavily wooded meadowland and aimed, as always, to produce courses in which each hole would have individuality. Many of his holes are at least slightly dog-legged, being to left or right impartially. Deep bunkers hug most of the greens closely. Tillinghast considered that one of the greatest merits of a golf course was that it demanded accuracy for the shots into the greens, and Winged Foot is very testing in this respect. He gave as much attention to the green approaches as to any other features of the course, so that shots that are just not quite good enough tend to be thrown aside into the greenside bunkers. The greens themselves are subtly contoured and, at championship pitch, are both hard and bewilderingly fast. The rough can be very severe – particularly when the course is being set up for championship play – and in many places the trees pinch into the fairways.

Opened in 1923, the courses take their name from the club symbol of the New York Athletic Club. The US Open has come to Winged Foot West on four occasions, and all four championships have been memorable in one way or another.

The first, in 1929, saw Bobby Jones at both his best and his worst. He began with a flawless 69 to establish a grasp on the championship, and seemed to be cruising to an easy victory when he parred the opening holes in his final round. But this situation exemplified Jones's Achilles' heel: he tended to lose concentration when the job seemed to be done. On the 8th, he bunkered his shot to the green and then exploded out into another bunker across the green.

He repeated the performance to finish with a triple-bogey 7 on the hole. He then returned to steady golf, and with four holes to play had only to par in to win by three strokes. Easy. Jones immediately made things difficult by taking 7 on the next hole, a par 4. He then three-putted the 70th. If he could achieve two pars on the final holes, however, he could at least tie. Jones got the first with no problem but missed the green on the 18th and then pitched to 12 feet (3·5 m) or so. The putt had considerable borrow, but Jones was nevertheless able to sink it.

He was into a play-off with Al Espinosa, a man who had played the last half-dozen holes beautifully and without a care in the world – he was sure that the 8 he had just scored on the 12th had given Jones the championship. The next day, Jones went out and shot rounds of 72 and 69 to win by 23 strokes, a record 36-hole play-off margin. The wonder is how Jones managed that second round of 69 once he knew the title was already well and truly in the bag.

It was exactly 30 years before the championship returned, in 1959. This contest has not become part of golfing legend, but it is remembered, at least in part, because the champion, Billy Casper, single-putted 31 greens. In 1959, his total of only 114 putts was thought amazing. Few eyebrows would be raised today.

In 1974, the course beat the players. It could be said that no one won, but that Hale Irwin lost less than the other players! His total of 287 was 7 over par. The high scoring was the result not of difficult weather but of the severity of the course. Jack Nicklaus considered that, if players had to compete on Winged Foot most of the time, they might learn to drive and putt much better. Gary Player thought it the greatest US Open test he had ever played – but then Gary makes remarks in the superlative nearly all the time.

The selection of Winged Foot West by the USGA only 10 years later showed that the course was rated very highly. This time, two players did beat the course, Fuzzy Zoeller and Greg Norman, who were both 4 under par when

they tied for the championship. On the last hole Norman, playing just ahead of Zoeller, holed one of the great putts of championship history. The hole was set in the same spot as when Jones had won back in 1929, but Norman was some 40 feet (12 m) away with about 4 feet (1·2 m) of break on his putt. Back down the fairway, Zoeller thought Norman had birdied the hole and picked up a towel and waved it to signal surrender.

That play-off, as with Jones versus Espinosa, was one-way, with Zoeller's 8-stroke margin being a record for an 18-hole play-off in the US Open.

It is the severity of the par 4s, with 10 well over 400 yards (365 m) long for the Open, which impresses one at Winged Foot. Perhaps the best is the 17th at 444 yards (406 m), which doglegs gently right and demands a long-iron second shot of great precision between the bunkers to the long and narrow green.

The 10th is a famous par 3. Tillinghast considered the green the best he ever constructed. Although the bunkers set in the upslope to this elevated green are both large and deep, the subtle undulations on the putting surface are the hole's best defence.

ABOVE The splendid 1920s clubhouse at Winged Foot with the 9th green in the foreground.

LEFT A W Tillinghast, the creator of many top-class US golf courses, designed the two present courses at Winged Foot. They were finally opened in 1923 and the West course hosted the US Open for the first time in 1929.

● SELECT BIBLIOGRAPHY ●

ALLEN, PETER *Play the Best Courses,* 1973

ALLISS, PETER AND HOBBS, MICHAEL *The Good Golf Guide,* 1986

BRAID, JAMES *Advanced Golf,* 1908

COLT, H S AND ALISON, C H *Some Essays on Golf Course Architecture,* 1920

CORNISH, GEOFFREY S AND WHITTEN, RONALD E *The Golf Course,* 1981

DARWIN, BERNARD *Golf Courses of the British Isles,* 1910

DARWIN, BERNARD *Golf on the LNER,* 1924

DAVIS, WILLIAM H *Great Golf Courses of the World,* 1974

DICKINSON, PATRICK *A Round of Golf Courses,* 1951

Golfer's Handbook, The 1898–1988

Golfing Annual, The 1888–1910

HAWTREE, F W *The Golf Course: Planning, Design, Construction and Maintenance,* 1983

HOBBS, MICHAEL *The Golfer's Companion,* 1988

HUNTER, ROBERT *The Links,* 1926

HUTCHINSON, HORACE *British Golf Links,* 1897

HUTCHINSON, HORACE AND OTHERS *Famous Golf Links,* 1891

JENKINS, DAN *The Best 18 Golf Holes in America,* 1966

JONES, ROBERT TRENT, *Golf Course Architecture,* 1936

LAWLESS, PETER *The Golfer's Companion,* 1937

LYLE, SANDY AND FERRIER, BOB *The Championship Courses of Scotland,* 1982

MCCORMACK, MARK H *The World of Professional Golf,* 1967–1988

MACDONALD, C B *Scotland's Gift: Golf,* 1928

MACKENZIE, DR ALISTER *Golf Architecture,* 1920, 1982

MILLER, DICK *America's Greatest Golfing Resorts,* 1977

PARK, WILLIE *The Game of Golf,* 1896

PENNINK, FRANK *Choice of Golf Courses,* 1976

PRICE, CHARLES *The World of Golf,* 1962

RAMSEY, TOM *Twenty-Five Great Australian Golf Courses,* 1981

RYDE, PETER AND STEEL, DONALD *The Shell International Encyclopedia of Golf,* 1975

SCOTT, TOM (ed) *The AA Guide to Golf in Great Britain,* 1977

THOMAS, GEORGE *Golf Architecture in America,* 1927

WARD-THOMAS, PAT (ed) *The World Atlas of Golf,* 1977

WETHERED, H N AND SIMPSON, TOM *The Architectural Side of Golf,* 1929

WIND, HERBERT WARREN *The Complete Golfer,* 1954

WIND, HERBERT WARREN *Following Through,* 1985

WIND, HERBERT WARREN *The Lure of Golf,* 1971

(The many golf club histories published often contain material on individual courses)

The author would like to acknowledge that invaluable reference work, *The Golf Course* by Geoffrey S Cornish and Ronald E Whitten (Rutledge Press, 1981). Listings of courses and birth and death dates have often been invaluable.

INDEX